Georgestown

National Library of Canada Cataloguing in Publication

Furlong, Wallace, 1918-2000
    Georgestown : an historic corner of St. John's / Wallace Furlong.

ISBN 1-894463-23-4

    1. Georgestown (St. John's, N.L.)--History. 2. Georgestown (St. John's,
N.L.)--Biography. 3. St. John's (N.L.)--History. 4. St. John's (N.L.)--Biography.
I. Title.

FC2196.52.F87 2004   971.8'1   C2003-906828-5

Cover photo: Tooton's
Courtesy of Ed Murphy

Cover photo: Basilica of St. John the Baptist
Courtesy of Maura Hanrahan

PRINTED IN CANADA BY FRIESENS CORPORATION

FLANKER PRESS LTD.
P.O. BOX 2522, STATION C
ST. JOHN'S, NL
CANADA
A1C 6K1
TOLL FREE: 1-866-739-4420
TELEPHONE: (709) 739-4477
FAX: (709) 739-4420
INFO@FLANKERPRESS.COM
WWW.FLANKERPRESS.COM

Canada

We acknowledge the financial support of the Government of Canada through the
Book Publishing Industry Development Program (BPIDP) for our publishing program.

Georgestown

AN HISTORIC CORNER OF OLD ST. JOHN'S

by Wallace Furlong

Flanker Press Ltd.
St. John's, NL
2004

Contents

Foreword by Tom Furlong

I: Introduction 1

II: Rebuilding 3

III: Origin of the Name Monkstown 6

IV: Tubridstown: The Compact Community 11

V: Garages & Auto Distributor Establishments 14

VI: Commercial Enterprise in Georgestown 23

VII: Michael Kearney:

      Newfoundland's Greatest Shipbuilder 45

VIII: The Avalon Athletic Club 50

IX: The General Protestant Academy 59

X: The Private Schools of Georgestown 64

XI: Belvedere 71

XII: St. Bonaventure's: Newfoundland's First College 85

XIII: The New York Circus Comes to St. John's 95

XIV: The Grand Old Man of Georgestown 100

XV: The Dutch Painter of Georgestown 109

XVI: The Conspiracy That Failed 116

XVII: The Georgestown Lad Who Retired at Age 30 123

XVIII: The Georgestown Pilot:

    Newfoundland's First Aviator 132

XIX: The Railway Accident in Georgestown 139

XX: The Barnes Family of Georgestown 143

XXI: More About the Barnes Family 149

XXII: Captain Cleary: The Plimsoll of Newfoundland 158

XXIII: The Famous Mitchell's Gardens 164

Foreword

Wallace Furlong was born at 24 Allandale Road, which is now 72 Bonaventure Avenue, and lived there most of his life. He was the sixth child of Edward T. Furlong and Annie Healy. There were nine of us, six boys and three girls. When we moved there from Pennington Cottage on Irwin's Road, we were still regarded as "living in the country." The City Limits were a mere stone's throw away from our northern fence, which was on The Old Track, now known as Empire Avenue. Pennington Cottage was the last building to be demolished when Memorial University was built. It was only a few yards east of Bowater House and about the same distance from the road. It served as a psychology lab for some years.

We caught trout, with our bare hands, in Kelly's Brook, sailed boats—and got generally wet—in Coughlan's Gully, skated and played hockey on Duder's Bog, all now covered over. The Lions Club chalet sits on Coughlan's Gully, Churchill Park covers Duder's Bog, and Kelly's Brook is culverted from the Gully to Rennie's Mill Road.

Wallace was ambidextrous, predominately left-handed, a trait which came in handy when he had to write "I can do better" a hundred times in school. We never asked how he kept his scribbler straight while he was writing these lines. He was a better than average student and played hockey well enough to get his name on the Boyle Trophy twice. After we all went to work and got "proper jobs," he turned our potato patch into a flower garden that was the envy of many. (Oh yes, we grew our own vegetables, had a cow which kept us in milk and hens to keep us from buying eggs.)

He could, as the saying goes, turn his hand to anything. He worked in the Parts Department at E.O'D. Kelly's Garage and Whelan's Garage before he went to Fort Pepperrell, where he was employed in the Maintenance Department with responsibility for ensuring that all contracts were properly carried out. After Pepperrell he became a Land Surveyor and worked on many construction projects, some of which took him to the remotest parts of the Island.

He was not exactly a world traveller. He got as far east as Scotland and as far west as California and rode in the Pace Car at the Indy 500, though not on the day of the Race.

Wallace was always interested in the history of the City of St. John's, especially the lesser-known incidents. One of the forges he mentions in this work is Hamlyn's. For a number of years we had a pony, and since 10 Belvedere Street was no distance from 24 Allandale Road, it was only natural that we took our steed to Mr. Hamlyn when he needed new shoes.

Wallace was a great rooter. He had the patience of Job, and when he took on a task, nothing was too much trouble to get all the facts. When he was preparing his article on Sir James Pearl, he wrote the British Admiralty in London, asking for clarification on a certain point. The Chief Archivist there told him he knew more about the famous captain than they did. In his last years he was working on the story of the SS *Waverly*, a ship famous for having had its upper deck converted into a dance hall and transported to a location on Topsail Road.

His attention to detail is well exemplified in this history of Georgestown, which was first published in serial form in *The*

Seniors News. It has a wealth of information on the area. The present residents are living on "hallowed ground." There were industries, commercial enterprises, a cathedral and a college (the last two are still there), and some famous people called it Home.

Thomas E. Furlong

* Note to reader: The stories contained herein were written within a two-year period, from May 1980 when the "Introduction" was penned, to May of 1982 when the last story, "The Famous Mitchell Gardens," was first put to paper.

W.J. Murphy Ltd., family grocer, at the corner of Monkstown and Military Roads, has continually served the neighbourhood with top-quality produce since 1915. (Courtesy of Ed Murphy)

I

Introduction

Early St. John's grew along the harbourfront, the early settlers making their homes over their business premises, or as near
as possible to the varied trades places that were so closely tied to
the fishing industry that brought the adventurous West Country
of England merchants and their employees to the New-Found-
Land of Cabot's voyage of discovery.

As years went by and permanent settlement was finally
made possible by legal means, the influx of immigrants pushed
the town's boundaries back from the harbour shoreline. The new
arrivals began to build on the outer areas adjoining the already
overcrowded town; the expansion was up over the north slope
and out through the valleys. In turn, future generations established the neighbourhoods or small boroughs of Hoylestown,
Riverhead, Maggoty Cove, Waterford Bridge Valley, Quidi Vidi,
Southside, King's Bridge, Higher Levels, Freshwater Valley, The
Battery, Mundy Pond, Tubridstown, Monkstown and
Georgestown. These, added to the original East End and West
End, comprised the old St. John's.

Over the years, since the time of the first settlement, the old
city has been scarred by fires, plundered and sacked by invaders
and pirates, and had its share of civil strife, mutiny and rioting;
but the fire of 1892 was the most devastating of all, as it wiped
out more than 70 per cent of the homes and business establish-

ments in town. However, like the famed Phoenix of mythology, St. John's arose, once more, from the ashes and ruins of that great conflagration, and the small boroughs began to grow and emerge in time. It was through an act of God, in the form of a change in the direction of the wind, that Georgestown, the first of the strictly residential districts, and its adjacent neighbourhoods of Monkstown and the Tubridstown, escaped the all-consuming flames of the disastrous fire.

That section of St. John's now known as the Georgestown Neighbourhood Improvement Area is made up of what was formerly three separate towns, several large estates and many small fields. They were: George Winter's Village, the oldest; James Tobin's subdivision; and James Tubrid's compact community. The area is bounded by Military Road, Bonaventure Avenue, Empire Avenue and Monkstown Road.

Winter's Village was the first residential neighbourhood, dating back to 1819, and became known as Georgestown. Tobin's property, which was quite extensive, was laid out as a subdivision shortly after the fire of 1846. It was named Monkstown. Tubrid's community consisted of neat clusters of homes. It was located between the Barnes estate, Presentation Convent and St. Bonaventure's College properties on the west, and Monkstown on the east. This little neighbourhood was settled around 1840, and was called "Tubridstown." The only street entrance was through Barnes Laneway, until Tobin's subdivision came into existence.

The estates and fields in the area were used as one of the main sources for the supply of local items of agriculture. Animal grains and hay were cultivated in the larger fields. The estate of Emerson, "Belvedere" was in all probability the biggest and best farm in the neighbourhood. Hugh Emerson was a descendant of an Empire Loyalist who settled in Nova Scotia after the U.S. War of Independence. Hugh and his brothers George and Lewis came to St. John's, where they built estates on the outskirts of town.

Mr. William Irwin's fields were mainly used as grazing ranges for cattle and horses, but he cultivated cattle grains and hay in several of them for a supply of livestock feeds. The smaller properties were used to produce staple vegetables to supply the families of the owners with food throughout the winter and spring seasons.

II

Rebuilding

Following the fires of 1818 (two fires within a month), a group of the townspeople, those of better circumstances, appointed a committee (from the group) to locate a suitable site for a proposed residential village that would be away from the clustered section of the town, but near enough to be part of St. John's. The delegation approached a Mr. George Winter with the intent of purchasing some of his land in order to proceed with their proposed village. In the opinion of the committee, Winter's land would be the ideal location for their residential community. It was approximately five acres in area, and situated high on the south slope of a dale about 1,000 feet to the north beyond the military road connecting Fort William with Fort Townshend.

This road was built along the ridge on the north slope of St. John's harbour, and ran along an east-west direction. Only a few cottages, meadows and barrens were between the military road and that portion of Winter's land that the group was interested in purchasing, separating the site from the old town. Access to this proposed residential village would be over a trail to plantations and farms in the upper Long Pond locality. The military also used this trail to man the Queen Victoria Hills fortifications. The proposed village would be completely safe from fire should St. John's suffer such disasters as had been experienced in the years 1817 and 1818.

*

After several meetings with George Winter, the land was made available, either through leasing or outright purchasing, and within the next few years (1820-21) the residential village became a reality. Planned lanes in the form of public ways, with cottages set in neat, well-kept gardens on both sides of the roadway, gave access from one place to another without trespassing a neighbour's property. All homes had private wells in their yards or under the house, but there were several water tanks (wooden) and a few public wells located throughout the neighbourhood. These were for firefighting purposes, and they were regularly checked by appointed residents in order to be sure of a supply of water at all times should a fire break out within the community.

The first residents were James Vinlay, Duncan MacPhee, William Dalton, George Tillmann, James Aide and Henry MacDonald. They were soon followed by new immigrants from the British Isles, and by 1830 the village extended from Donnelly's Lane to what is now Belvedere Street. MacPhee moved to Nova Scotia and Tillmann went to Brooklyn, N.Y., where he died in 1854. A Mr. P. Tarrahan occupied a small house where Fleming Street now meets Monkstown Road. In the year 1921-22, the property was purchased to widen the Fleming Street-Monkstown Road junction. Mr. J. Johnston purchased the house from the council and tore it down. The wood was in such good condition that he built a barn and workshop from the board and studding on an Allandale Road site, in the vicinity of Burton's Pond, almost 100 years after the materials had been originally used in the construction of a fine home. Tarrahan, who was a bachelor, inherited the house from his uncle. He then moved to McDougall Street, where he resided with his sister, a spinster, who was also given her home by the same uncle.

*

When people moved into the village from the old town, the word was passed around in that part of St. John's, where the family formerly lived, that they had migrated to Georgestown. This was not a slur or reference toward the people who had moved out, nor was it looked upon as an elevation to a social level, but just a casual remark to explain the new residential address of the family. Within a short period of time, the new community became known as Georgestown, and it has retained that name to the present day.

There are two or three old houses located on the south side of Fleming Street that date back to about 1885. They were not part of the original village houses, but they were built on one of the early public lanes of the old community. There were several old foundations along old Donnelly's Lane that were removed when a modern service station was erected in that area more than 15 years ago. Three or more old homes fronting on Monkstown Road were part of the original village, having been built between 1830 and 1860. Most of these houses have now been rebuilt and only remotely resemble the early cottages.

There was one duplex house of the original village, built in 1820-21, but was torn down in the mid-1930s to widen Hayward Avenue at its junction with Fleming Street. It was then occupied by Mr. Nelson Helpand and family in the south half, and by Mr.

Robert Bellmore and family in the north half. The houses or homes were the very essence of antiquity; they had double-hung windows, and the roofs were wood-shingled. The second floor was built into the rock with dormer-type windows to permit natural light into the rooms. Although the building had water and sewage services, electric services were not connected, and on winter nights, one could see the occupant moving from room to room carrying oil lamps. The ceilings were no more than seven feet in height, and both dwellings had open-hearth fireplaces. The tenants were always comfortable within the cottages, at all times. The garden had rustic fences built in diamond-pattern style, and huge broadleaf sycamore trees completely shaded the houses in summertime. The winter season appearance of this fine old duplex cottage could very well pass for the setting of a Currier and Ives Christmas Card.

III

Origin of the Name Monkstown

It should be here noted that Monkstown Road (east side) and Bonaventure Avenue (formerly Allandale Road) were outside the boundaries of Georgestown. However, both are now incorporated within the Neighbourhood Improvement Plan area; in the case of Bonaventure Avenue, only to where it crosses Empire Avenue (formerly the old Railway [Nfld.] right-of-way) but including all homes on this avenue, east to its junction with Carpasian Road. Therefore, old buildings, historic sites, estates, public figures, etc. will be included in this brief historical outline of Monkstown.

*

The name "Monkstown," with relation to the settlement of that portion of land in the south and east sector of Georgestown, is derived from the town of Monkstown, which is now a suburb of Dublin, Ireland.

James Tobin, an immigrant from Monkstown to St. John's, established the shipping firm of J. Tobin & Co., through which he accumulated a fortune. Tobin obtained a grant to a tract of land north of the Military Road connecting Fort William with Fort Townshend. The land granted Tobin was bounded on the east by the trail that led to Georgestown, beyond to the plantations and farms, in the Upper Long Pond region and the Queen Victoria Hills fortifications. This grant was obtained sometime between the years 1843 and 1846 and was considered quite extensive at that time. Other citizens, Mrs. Greene, Mr. Tubrid, Mr. Boyd, Mrs. Tappin, Mr. Barnes and Mr. Duggan all sought and obtained grants for land in the area adjacent to Military Road, but west of Tobin's grant.

James Tobin (later Sir James) was appointed to the Amalgamated House by the Crown in the year 1843, and later became a member of the Legislative Council when Responsible Government (Home Rule) was granted to Newfoundland in the year 1855.

It was during this era (1835-1850) that another immigrant, Mr. J. Noad, from Upper Canada but by way of Nova Scotia, came to St. John's. Noad, like Tobin, was also appointed by the Crown to serve in the Amalgamated House. Noad was the Surveyor General, and a very close friend of James Tobin. It was the Surveyor General who designed the property layout of streets for Tobin several years after the Great Fire of 1846.

Although Tobin did not build a home on his land grant, he named the area "Monkstown Meadows" as a monument to the town of his birthplace in Ireland. In the early 1830s, there were several cottages just off the Upper Long Pond Trail. The Harris Cottage, built in 1833, is in excellent condition today. Built by William Harris 147 years ago, this fine old house is now occupied by his great-granddaughter. The Haddon Cottage, now owned by Mr. H. Buckingham, has been recently renovated, but structurally it is virtually the same in its external appearance. The Thompson Cottage, at one time the residence of William Carson, was torn down in the year 1956 when Mr. Caule purchased the property. He built a modern two-storey house on the site. In the subdivision, Tobin named the streets after members of his family: Catherine, James and William. However, James was later renamed Mullock Street in honour of the R.C. Bishop, his friend and pastor. This street appears to be the only named monument for the great prelate, but the most famous landmark that His Lordship is remembered by is St. Bonaventure's College.

Although Tobin's "Monkstown" meadows or fields were an extensive undertaking for real estate at that time, it was not until well into the 1860s that his dream of the early 1850s began to fill up with new home construction. Most of the new homes were built along the north side of James (Mullock) Street at first, and then along the south side of William Street. Nearly all of them were erected by William Harris, a master carpenter and distant relative of Tobin.

Tobin's "Monkstown Meadows," that zone between James (Mullock) Street and Catherine Street bounded by Hayward Avenue, was open space in 1859 when he tried to interest the government to lease it forever at a fee of 50 pounds sterling per annum, as the site for the proposed home for the aged and infirm.

The wealthy merchant and shipping magnate was no longer in the government, and his offer of perpetual leasing was rejected, even though the site was considered the ideal location because of its nearness to the downtown and of its proximity to the various denominational churches of St. John's. It would also have brought about an immediate end to the "eyesore" known as "The Camps": the temporary shelters erected on the parade grounds of Fort Townshend that had housed the fire victims of the conflagration of 1846, and which was still in use to accommodate the destitute and poor of the city.

There is also another theory regarding the origin of the name Monkstown within the old city of St. John's. A farmer or plantation owner named Monk had deeds to a large tract of land for farming purposes situated on the present Monkstown Road and bounded on the east by Crown lands (Rennie's Mill Road and Bannerman Park in later years). When the family got too old to cultivate the land, it became available for homes construction, and thus the settlement grew and was named after the original owner.

There is a small public way that leads off present-day Monkstown Road called Monk's Lane. When searching through old deeds for land grants, no such properties could be located that were made out to any Monk family in the area. However, there is a map dated 1806 showing a large plantation property situated between present-day Rennie's Mill and Monkstown Roads that gives support to the assumption that the name "Monkstown" was called after the Monk family.

Yet another belief is that the name Monkstown originated when, in 1847, Bishop Fleming opened a Third Order of Monks (Franciscans Teaching Brothers) at Belvedere. The Order consisted of laymen who were permitted to use the brown habit of the Franciscans, but were not bound by religious orders. Because the monks were housed in Belvedere and in the new town, the name "Monkstown" came about.

Harris Cottage, 43 Monkstown Road
One of the oldest dwellings in St. John's, Harris Cottage managed
to survive two of the Great Fires that ravaged the city during the
nineteenth century. The house was built in 1833 by William
Harris, who moved to St. John's from Ferryland in 1832. One of
the earliest identifiable builders in St. John's, Harris was a carpenter and master builder who was responsible for many of the
houses in Georgestown. His son, also called William, followed in
his father's footsteps, becoming a master builder himself. He is
also credited with building many of the houses in the area. It was
designated as a Registered Heritage Structure by the Heritage
Foundation of Newfoundland and Labrador in April 1990.
(Courtesy of the Heritage Society of Newfoundland and
Labrador)

It is, therefore, reasonable to assume that the first version is the true origin of the name "Monkstown," which is a large portion of the settlement of Georgestown in old St. John's.

IV

Tubridstown: The Compact Community

The neat little community known as Tubridstown (that portion of land that is today bounded by Mullock Street, Hayward Avenue, the Unnamed Street and Barnes Road) was founded in the year 1840, when James Tubrid had a range of ten houses built on the land he had obtained by grant in the year 1817.

James Tubrid came to St. John's in the year 1809 and set up his business in premises he had leased that were on the harbour waterfront. Although the property was small, it had a wharf located in deep water which afforded access for alongside loading of ships for his product, which he sold to the fishery trade. Tubrid was a master cooper, and his skill in the manufacture of barrels, kegs and other wooden items used in the packing and shipping of cured fishing produce soon became the choice of all the exporters of dried and cured fish.

At first James Tubrid lived in a house he had leased, from a William Hogan, in Maggoty Cove. When the short-term lease expired, Tubrid then moved to Military Road where he leased a cottage from Sophia Green (this cottage was located between present-day Barnes Road and the corner where Monkstown Road meets Military Road—W.J. Murphy's Grocery Store Corner).

It was while residing here that Tubrid became acquainted with the problems that William Barnes experienced with the general public, and garrison soldiers in particular, crossing over the back area of his property. The path that they made caused many repairs to his fences and a source of continued disputes with the military and public who used this route as a "short cut" to get them to Georgestown Road (now called Monkstown Road), rather than go by way of Military Road. In the year 1837, Tubrid leased this section of the Barnes property, including the part on which the troublesome path crossed over. He used the "path problem" to reduce the cost while bargaining the lease price, and also the conditions, which were now all in his favour.

When the agreements were settled and duly signed by both parties, Tubrid hired a carpenter to build three larger houses fronting the north side of the path which separated his leasehold property from that of William Barnes. The first house completed became the residence of James and Elizabeth Tubrid, and their two daughters, Margaret and Bridget. The second, upon completion, was leased to a Martin Carew, who was a close relative, and the third one was leased to a Mary Anne Maloney, who opened a rooming establishment there.

When Bishop Fleming secured, by grants, the old Williams Plantation (which was used as a woodshed for the garrison at Fort Townshend) in the year 1836, he had Fr. Troy arrange for and supervise the building of a strong wooden fence to enclose the approximate ten acres of land, on which a cathedral, convents, clergy residence, schools and graveyard were to be built, bringing an end to the "path" that caused William Barnes such annoyance. Tubrid leased the remaining portion of his land along the dead-end path which could only be entered through Barnes Lane. Within the year, Tubrid named the "path" Cathedral Lane. The name was changed to Carew Avenue in or around the year

1875. Shortly after 1900, it was once more renamed, this time to Barnes Place, by which it is known today. Tubrids Cooperage, his lumber (import) company, his seven farm grants (each not less than 20 acres in size), the numerous small land grants in and around old St. John's, leased to farmers and immigrants for homes construction, helped to make him a very wealthy man.

In the year 1840 he hired carpenters to build a range or row of small houses on his land grant situated at the back end of Barnes Lane. When this range of houses was completed, he leased them to British Isles immigrants in St. John's. Most were occupied by Irishmen from Cork and Wexford. The response for housing was so great that he then leased land in this area to those who had the means to construct their own homes. However, he had another small range of houses built along a lane at the back of his first range of houses. He referred to this new range as being located on the Back Lane. The Back Lane is today the part of Hayward Avenue between Mullock Street and the Unnamed Street.

The first range of ten houses that James Tubrid had built in his community was generally known as the "Ten Commandments" during the early decades of this century. Even when there were only five remaining units of the original ten houses in the year 1933, they still retained that name. Later in the year, they were torn down and replaced by modern two-storey houses. All the old houses of Tubridstown have been replaced, even though some of the replacements date back to the year 1876. However, it is possible that some parts, such as basements, could still be found in the old neighbourhood.

James Tubrid died August 3, 1861, almost four years after his wife, Elizabeth, passed away (Sept. 19, 1857). They were buried in Belvedere Cemetery. Of his family, Margaret, the elder daughter, married a Thomas Murphy, by whom she had a son named James. Thomas Murphy died August 12, 1865. Margaret remarried three years later to a widower, a Cornelius Callahan, who was a son of Callahan of Callahan Glass Co., manufacturers and importers of furniture; their premises were located where the Majestic Building now stands, at the junction of Duckworth, New Gower Streets and Queen's Road. Margaret (Tubrid) Callahan died July 4, 1872, and is buried alongside her mother and father in Belvedere Cemetery. Her son James Murphy died October 18, 1884, and is buried in the same cemetery.

Bridget Tubrid married a Captain Charles Allen, who died at St. Jago, in the Lesser Antilles, Caribbean Sea on January 9, 1872.

Bridget had two children: James, named after his grandfather, died at sea on October 5, 1885; Margaret, named after her aunt, married a Walter Barnes. She died at St. John's on January 11, 1875. Bridget (Tubrid) Allen died at St. John's, August 15, 1875. All the Allen family are buried in the Allen plot in Belvedere Cemetery.

V

Garages & Auto Distributor Establishments

The motor car industry (as it was then named) got an early start in St. John's, about the year 1908-09. At that time, residents of great wealth would go to Great Britain and purchase motor cars, use them while there, and then have them shipped to St. John's. Such famous brand names as Rolls Royce, Daimler, Bently, Sunbeam and others were familiar to the citizens of old St. John's by the year 1910-11.

As there were no authorized sales and no service garages here to make necessary repairs if cars developed mechanical failures, the manufacturers sent chauffeurs (drivers) out from their factories with each motor car. The man, if not already a mechanic, was given six weeks' intensive training in basic mechanical repair methods and driving lessons. The driving lessons included a course in Motor Act Rules and Regulations of the country to which the motor car was to be exported by the manufacturer. Customs clearance procedures of vehicles and spare-or-replacement parts were also included in the course that the chauffeurs were given before they left Great Britain in charge of the exported cars. Many young men of Great Britain were trained in this manner, and all the major car manufactures had an ample supply of chauffeurs on hand for immediate car export.

In the year 1910, a Mr. Fred J. Dodd came to St. John's under this chauffeur-mechanic policy. Dodd was born in Liverpool, but when his father died the family moved to the Isle of Man, in England, where he spent his boyhood. As a young lad of 16 years, he went to Wolverhampton and there apprenticed as a motor mechanic at the Rolls Royce Motor Works. He came with a Rolls Royce motor car for a Mr. Grant, merchant and fur ranch or farm owner of St. John's. Mr. Grant had gone to London on business and, while there, met a Mr. W.D. Reid, co-owner and builder of the Reid Newfoundland Railway. They both purchased motor cars at the London sales offices of the Rolls Royce Motor Works. They were casually invited to visit the factory at Wolverhampton to see the assembly of Rolls Royce motor cars. The two men went there to see the marvels of car manufacture. The assembly foreman was Mr. Fred Dodd.

Mr. Grant and Mr. Reid were so impressed with the man's ability and his direction and supervision of the men of his work crew that they asked that Mr. Dodd be one of the chauffeurs to accompany the cars which they purchased to St. John's. The request was granted, and Mr. Dodd, having agreed to go along, selected a man named Weatherlee as the other chauffeur. However, after approximately six months, Weatherlee returned to Great Britain and within a few weeks sailed to Victoria, Australia as a chauffeur with a Rolls Royce for a wealthy family, MacPherson-Robertson by name, residing in Melbourne. It should be noted that Fred Dodd was a bona fide mechanic trained at the Rolls Royce Motor Works in Wolverhampton and not a trainee under the Chauffeur-Basic Mechanics School.

In the year 1911, Mr. Dodd sought and obtained the Ford Motor Car Agency for Newfoundland. Early in the following year, he took over a feed-storage shed and stable for horses on Catherine Street and began the rebuilding of the premises into a modern motor car garage for the display, sales and services of Ford motor cars in particular, and of the motor car trade in general, of St. John's. His garage had showrooms fronting on Catherine Street, while the entry to the oil-and-lubricating facilities and paint shop was from Gorman's Lane at the rear of the building. Later in the same year, he constructed a new car paint shop at the east section of the garage, which housed the first auto spray-painting shop in Newfoundland that was equipped with compressed air-spray painting guns and electric-lamp drying apparatus. Although the establishment was named the Central Garage, it was generally known as Dodd's Garage to the public.

In 1913, Mr. Dodd married Mollie Burden, the eldest daughter of a merchant planter of Salvage. Mr. Burden owned and operated an inshore fishing fleet of small schooners and skiffs around the shores of the Eastport peninsula and had fishing rooms and stations along the coast of Labrador where his larger schooners operated during the fishing season. He also owned a small sawmill operation in the Eastport area.

In 1913, Dodd brought out several factory-trained motor car mechanics from Great Britain for his garage in Georgestown of St. John's. He also hired several chauffeur-mechanics who now made St. John's their home. Added to this basic staff he apprenticed young men of St. John's. Mr. Fred Smeaton, a master mechanic, was the garage foreman and a Mr. Irvine was his shops motor car electrician. (Smeaton was a direct relation of Britain's Queen Mother, a fact brought to light by J.R. Smallwood, former Premier of Newfoundland.)

Early in the year 1919, Mr. Dodd was in Great Britain to finalize a sale of Fords he had somehow engineered in England. While there, he went into a Rolls Royce Motor Works in Wolverhampton. The visit was in connection with the Rolls Royce Eagle aeroplane engines that were to be used in a Vickers Vimy plane that would shortly be shipped to St. John's for a Captain John Alcock and Lieutenant A.W. Brown, who were entries in the Trans-Atlantic Air Race. The engines came to Dodd's garage in St. John's. Some of the work of the engine assembly was done in the Central Garage, but most of it took place in a makeshift hangar at Quidi Vidi lakeside, from where the Vickers Vimy plane flew to Lester's Field, the takeoff site of what was to be an historic event in the history of aviation. When the engines were assembled and mounted in the Vickers Vimy aeroplane, and as Mr. Dodd did or supervised most of the mechanical assembly, the story has it that both Alcock and Brown insisted that he (Dodd) should go along on the test flight. It was said that Brown placed the leather helmet on Dodd's head and Alcock adjusted the goggles to protect his eyes from the wind.

The flight test lasted for two hours. In that time they landed twice to make minor adjustments, but at no time other than these landings did the aeroplane fly below 2,000 feet altitude. There were several test flights prior to the June 16, 1919 takeoff of the Atlantic flight that brought fame and fortune to Captain Alcock and Lieutenant A.W. Brown and the British aircraft industry, and it is said that Dodd had some air time on them. The helmet and goggles that Dodd used were in possession of the Dodd family for a long time but over the years were lost in the usual way that many minor historic relics disappear, when families grow up and each member goes his or her separate way.

In 1923, Dodd went to New York to take delivery of an American LaFrance fire truck that he had sold to the Newfoundland government for the St. John's Fire Department. This was the first aerial-ladder fire truck to come to Newfoundland. When the fire truck arrived in Newfoundland, after check-out and cleanup, Mr. Dodd demonstrated it to the public on Water Street in front of the Court House. The ladder, fully extended and with a fireman at the top, was above the tower of the building.

The following year the Central Garage went bankrupt, and the mechanics were out of work. However, they were all so well trained by Dodd that none had any difficulty finding employment with other garages in St. John's. The building was vacant for almost three months, when three young machinists moved in and began a machine engineering works under the trade name of Cook & Ryall Ltd. A young machinist was a silent partner who did not want his name to appear over the firm's door or on the company stationery.

In the year of 1926, the Anglo-American Garage Company Ltd. was established under the management of a Mr. Joe Crocker, an Englishman who came out to St. John's with a Rolls Royce for a Taylor family of St. John's, sometime between 1919 and 1921. Crocker set up his garage on New Gower Street, at the corner of Military Road, but relocated to Catherine Street in the premises of the former Central Garage when it was vacated by the machine shop of Cook & Ryall Ltd., which dissolved partnership, and the principals of that firm opened businesses of their own in other sections of St. John's.

The Anglo-American Garage Company Ltd. were the sole agents and distributors for a variety of motor cars: the Graham Paige, Graham, Durant, Rugby, Jewett, and Mack trucks. For a while they were agents for White and Auto Car trucks, but their main sales were in automobiles rather than trucks and commercial vehicles. The firm did a brisk business up to the advent of the Depression and survived the lean years for a while, but in 1934 the lines of manufacture for which they were distributors were absorbed by bigger industrial giants, some of whom went bankrupt due to the Depression, and the fine old brand names faded from the markets.

Crocker's Garage was taken over by Newfoundland Tractor and Equipment Company Limited, and the shops were used as repair facilities and a parts and service centre for the famous Caterpillar tractor industrial and road-building equipment sold throughout Newfoundland.

In the year 1920 a young man, Edmund O'D. Kelly, just back from university, who had already been mechanically minded, opened a garage at the corner of Fleming Street and fronting on Donelly's Lane, with the dealership and distributor rights in Newfoundland for Chandler and Marmon motor cars. The following year he obtained the agency for Harley-Davidson and Indian motorcycles, which were big and powerful but highly manoeuvrable machines. He interested the Newfoundland Constabulary, who at that time were considering a Motorcycle Department for their Traffic Division, to invest in his vehicles. He offered to teach those selected as motorcycle policemen, and a staff of three mechanics and himself conducted the course for three months so that a backup force, as well as the original selectees, could carry out motor traffic control in the event regular operators were off on annual or sick leave. The Harley-Davidson product was the standard motorcycle used by the Constabulary up to 1934, and in 1950 it again became the vehicle of the Motorcycle Corps of the Newfoundland Constabulary.

In 1923, Kelly obtained the distributorship for the British motorcycle products Douglas, Triumph and Reading Standard, all lightweight- and medium-horsepower cycles. He had obtained the agency for the famous Henderson "Four" motorcycle the previous year. He now had the dealership for all the main motorcycle lines being manufactured in that era, and his sales were increasing yearly.

Mr. Kelly also built up his motor car line to keep pace with the rapid growth of the automobile trade in Newfoundland. He obtained the dealership for Hupmobile and the famous Stutz motor cars, and although he did not have the agency for Allis Chalmers, he imported and sold quite a few models of their manufacture.

He sold four Stutz 18-cylinder-engine motor cars to some very wealthy city residents on special orders, but that model was such an enormous gasoline user that it was not a very economical vehicle to sell in the Newfoundland marketplace. One such model used 45 gallons of gasoline to go and return from Harbour Grace. Even for a wealthy man, this motor car proved too expensive a luxury in those days.

In the year 1929, E.O'D. Kelly Ltd. took over the entire General Motors distribution from Bert Hayward Ltd. when the proprietor died in that year. Mr. Kelly built a big garage in the East End of St. John's. It fronted on both Duckworth and Water Streets, and had a side entrance to the middle floor from Hill O'Chips. He also built garages in Corner Book, Grand Falls and Carbonear for outlets for all products of General Motors, for which he now held exclusive distributorship in Newfoundland. His operation was the most successful garage business in the country, even up to the year 1950 when he relinquished the business and sold his garage in St. John's East End to Commercial Equipment Limited and retired from business completely. Mr. Kelly now resides at Waterford Bridge Road but spends his winters in St. Petersburg, Florida.

The old garage in which Kelly first started his auto distributor sales and service business was later taken over by Mr. Joe Mulrooney, who operated the 4158 Taxi Service, which was one of the most reliable and courteous taxi stands from the date of its inception in 1937 to 1953, when it closed out due to the failing health of the proprietor.

Mr. Mulrooney is presently employed as Bursar at Brother Rice Monastery, Bonaventure Avenue.

In 1954, the building on Fleming Street was taken over by a Mr. Russell, who conducted a very efficient auto body repair service under the trade name All Cars Auto Body Repair Shop. Although Mr. Russell no longer owns the shop, it still operates under the trade name he set up back in 1954.

Smeaton's Garage Ltd. opened for business in late 1925 or early 1926 and was located on Barnes Road in the premises formerly known as Tobin's Tyre Vulcanizing Garage. Smeaton had been the mechanical foreman at Fred J. Dodd's Central Garage on Catherine Street. (It should be noted that both buildings are bounded on the south by Gorman's Lane and are adjacent properties but facing different roads. However, the public right-of-way, Gorman's Lane, has recently been fenced off and apparently deeded over to the present owner of the building that held F.J. Dodd's Garage.)

Smeaton's Garage Ltd. was the sole agent and distributor sales and services outlet in Newfoundland for the Austin Motor

Car Works of Coventry in Great Britain. Fred Smeaton hired many of the mechanics who had worked under his direction when he was foreman at the old Central Garage of F.J. Dodd, most of whom he and Dodd had trained as auto mechanics under the apprenticeship training program inaugurated by Mr. Dodd when he opened his garage on Catherine Street in Georgestown. Smeaton hired young men and applied the same apprenticeship practice in his garage. Many young lads became qualified mechanics in due course. Mr. "Dick" Corbett and Mr. "Sandy" Fitzgerald, two young men who learned their trade from Smeaton, opened their own garage in other areas of St. John's in later years, and both were successful owners and operators up to the time of their deaths.

Smeaton ran his garage with great success, and sales of Austin motor cars were brisk up to 1931, when he closed down the premises under the trade name Smeaton's Garage Ltd., to take up a position with the Newfoundland Highroads Commission as the Mechanical Superintendent of Highways. His offices were located in the Highroad Garage, Bennett Avenue in St. John's, but his sphere of supervision of equipment and maintenance was the Dominion of Newfoundland, and he spent a good deal of his time travelling throughout the country in connection with the construction of our highway system.

Although Smeaton's Garage Ltd. was no longer the trade name of the garage on Barnes Road, the business continued operations under a Mr. Jack Ludlow, who now became the owner. He called the establishment Ludlow's Garage Ltd. Under the proprietor, the Austin Motor Car agency was retained and Ludlow had several years in sales, and several successful years in sales and services, with that popular product. In 1936, Ludlow relinquished his motor car agency and converted his business to a garage for general mechanical repairs for all makes of vehicles in the auto trade. Ludlow closed out his garage in 1938 and moved to Gander to take up position as Equipment Maintenance Superintendent at the Gander Airport. He later took a similar position at Goose Bay, where he worked up to the time of his death several years ago.

The garage building on Barnes Road was later taken over by a Mr. Michael Power, who renovated and enlarged the premises. He opened a modern service station with a two-bay grease-and-oil ramp service. His garage was successfully operated for many years. When he closed out the service station, he once again renovated the building and leased it to the Canadian Marconi Corporation, who used it as their Marine Division Department for sales and services of radar equipment.

Today the building houses the modern sporting goods outlet "Sports Beat" that has occupied the premises since its incorporation in 1976.

VI

Commercial Enterprise in Georgestown

Georgestown turned into a self-contained community from the original concept of a small residential village shortly after the Great Fire of St. John's in the year 1846.

Tubridstown and Monkstown Meadows rapidly filled up with new home construction, mostly on leased land, over the next 50 years as people moved out of the downtown area.

Many shops sprung up and grocery stores were numerous, with many streets having a "corner store," but most of the shops were situated along Hayward Avenue. This avenue was now the main thoroughfare of Georgestown.

It is interesting to note that, of all the grocery establishments that were doing business in the area, only W.J. Murphy Ltd., family grocer, at the corner of Monkstown and Military Roads, has continually served the neighbourhood with top-quality produce since 1915. Before that date, Mr. T.J. Edens built the store shortly after the Great Fire of 1892, and it was known as T.J. Edens, Family Grocer.

Mr. W.J. Murphy was trained as a druggist and worked for a short time with O'Mara's Drug Store, but he left that profession and went to work for Mr. Edens, where he learned the grocery-and-provisions trade. When Mr. Edens died in 1915, Mr. Murphy purchased the store from the Edens estate and renamed the business W.J. Murphy, Grocer (Successor to T.J. Edens).

Mr. Joe Murphy, his eldest son, who is now semi-retired, carried on the high-class grocery policy that was started by his father.

Mr. Ed Murphy, grandson of W.J., has recently taken over his father's (Joe) business and is operating a most efficient establishment while providing the high-class standards that have become a trademark of W.J. Murphy Ltd.

The neighbourhood had, at one time, five butcher, or meat, shops. The oldest was operated by a Mr. Miller. His place of business was located on the west side of Hayward Avenue. In the early 1920s, his was a thriving business and citizens frequented his shop because of the prompt and high-class service at all times. After the death of Mr. Miller, Mealey's Meat Market became the people's choice. This shop was also located on Hayward Avenue, and because of the central location in the neighbourhood, as well as his top-rate service and prime beef products, he got the bulk of the trade. Mr. Mealey died in the year 1930 and his meat market was closed down within weeks of his passing.

Eric and Ralph Clark operated the Dominion Meat Market located on the lower section of Belvedere Street, about opposite the old Newfoundland Brewery. The business was started in 1927 and provided produce and services to the area until 1933, when the brothers closed out. Ralph went to western Canada to purchase a cattle ranch whilst Eric took a position with the Newfoundland Post Office, where he worked until he retired.

Mr. Thompson had his meat market on Military Road about opposite Barnes Road where today a musical instrument sales centre is operated by Mr. Nichol. Mr. Thompson operated one of the best-kept meat markets in St. John's and his produce was of the highest quality at all times. Mr. Thompson died suddenly in 1934 and the business was closed almost immediately after his death.

In the early '30s, W.J. Murphy Ltd. built a meat market on the Monkstown side of their grocery store. They soon had the bulk of all the trade in Georgestown and the neighbouring areas, as they too operated a very clean and high-class business. In the late '60s they closed that market, but they still handle fresh meats as part of their grocery store operation.

Shoe repair shops dotted the neighbourhood in the years from 1900 to 1940. Shortall's Shoe Services set up a modern repair service in the year 1922 in the building vacated by Miller's Meat Market. Prior to this new location he had his repair shop on William Street where he started in business around the year 1907. Mr. Shortall had a very successful trade up to the time of his death in 1926. Shortall also repaired harnesses for horses and many of the neighbourhood cabmen availed of his services. The shop in which Shortall's Shoe Services had its glory days is now occupied by Mr. James Power and his sister "Kitty" who have the

A large tract of land owned by the Roman Catholic Church, bounded by what is now Mullock Street and Howley Avenue on one end and Bonaventure Avenue and Barnes Road on the other end, was open fields until the 1930s when many of the larger homes on these streets were constructed. This photo was taken from the roof of the Basilica looking northwest. (Courtesy of the Archives of the Roman Catholic Archdiocese c. 1925)

longest-standing confectionary store in Georgestown. Their mother started the business in 1928. Mr. Jim and Miss Kitty are, in all probability, the best-known shopkeepers in all the neighbourhood and are held in the highest esteem by everybody.

Mr. Kelly had his Shoe Repair Service on Barnes Road. He began business in 1912 and after his death in 1926 his sons carried on the operation until they retired in 1971. Theirs was a great service to the area and St. John's in general. The senior Kelly was a master craftsman in the art of shoemaking and he instructed his sons in the making and repairing of footwear. The Kellys made shoes to order and their clientele were from all classes of St. John's residents who wanted shoes made to measure. When Mr. Lewis Kelly retired, he closed down the firm his father had started 60 years previously; an era in the art of handmade shoemaking had thus come to an end in Georgestown.

Mr. George Myers opened a shoe repair shop on Catherine Street in 1930, which lasted until 1935. The following year Mr. John Constantine set up a shoe repair service at 16 Catherine Street. Mr. Constantine continued at that locality for another 11 years. As the old shop was to be torn down, Mr. Constantine purchased a house and shop at 3 Hayward Avenue and there carried on his shoe repair service and is still active in his business today, 44 years after he first opened for business.

Walter Day conducted a shoe repair service from his residence on Hayward Avenue for many years before he retired several years ago.

Trades were prominent in Georgestown before the turn of the century. Before the advent of the automobile (as we know it today), the horse and carriage was the means of transportation. The operators were known as cabmen or "cabbies," and gave a service that was most friendly at all times. A good number of the cab owners, who were also cabbies, lived in the area of Hayward

Avenue. John Carew had his stables at the east side of his home on Hayward Avenue and his garden, or court, with coach house was entered by way of what today is known as The Unnamed Street. In the garden, Carew had a well from which he watered his horse, washed his cab and did other tasks which required clean water. Carew was a relative of James Tubrid, the founder of Tubridstown. Carew's home and stable, with coach house, was built on land left to his father by Tubrid in 1863.

*

William Dinn lived on Hayward Avenue but entered his livery stables and coach houses from McDougall Street.

The Simmonds brothers, Art and Bill, lived on Barnes Road. Their stables were accessible from a lane that was entered from McDougall Street. Art owned a fine, chestnut-brown stallion and his brother Bill drove a big, white gelding. When customers called for a cab driven by the Simmondses, they would request either the brown Simmonds or the white Simmonds. Art, who owned the brown-coloured horse, also had a head covered with snow-white hair, while his brother's head was clad with hair of light brown. There was often confusion, but the fare always got good service as both men were of the most jovial character.

James Gladney operated out of his home on William Street. Entry to his stable and coach house was through a lane called "Wheelbarrow Lane." It got the name because it tapered down to about the width of a wheelbarrow about halfway through its length. On the end where Gladney entered to get to his stable the laneway was no more than 12 feet in width.

John Dodd lived on McDougall Street. His stables and coach house were at the rear of his home. Dodd was a most pleasant cabman and always kept his equipment in excellent condition. His cabs were painted black with gold scroll work. The coverings that protected his passengers from sun, rain or cold winds were made from the best materials and the rugs of the cab were of real fur (seal or bear) while the blankets were of pure wool, usually woven in Royal Stuart Tartan pattern.

Dodd was one of the first owners to provide his clients with a glass-windowed, closed-in coach for wintertime transportation. He hired a Mr. Lindsay to upholster the interior with red Morocco leather, covered and padded seats and had a system of hot bricks placed in the footrests so that his passengers would be warm and comfortable. His coaches were always spotless and shining on the outside and he himself dressed in the finest clothing which was patterned to that of the London cabbie of the 1890s. Dodd's property was left to his sister's children when he died at the grand age of 77. Dodd was the most popular of the cabmen in the height of the days of that era and style of transportation in old St. John's.

Where there were horses, there were also forges and blacksmiths. The blacksmith's trade was big business of which Georgestown had no less than four smithy's forges. They operated at full capacity until the early years of the third decade of the twentieth century.

Hamlyn's forge, located to the rear of the Hamlyn home on Belvedere Street, was torn down in 1953. Mr. Hamlyn learned his trade at Dougharty's in the west end of old St. John's. He worked for a short time with his brother, who had a forge on Prince's Street, but shortly after the Great Fire of 1892 he went into business on his own. His son, Robert Hamlyn, who resides at the old homestead on Belvedere Street, is also a blacksmith by trade and has most of the tools and forge equipment used by his father. It is believed to be stored in a shed at the rear of his home.

Bulger's Forge was located at the rear of the Bulger residence on Hayward Avenue and fronting on Bulger's Lane. In recent years the old forge was so vandalized that it had to be demolished in 1975 as it presented a hazard to the neighbour-hood. Ron Bulger took over the business from his father and did a very good trade up to around 1931 when he closed down the forge. Ron and his younger brother went to the Boston area where they both presently reside. Ron was a great lover of the sport and art of boxing, and in his off time would conduct lessons in the sport. He would set up a "ring" in the storeroom of his forge and have an amateur tournament there for the young lads of the immediate area. He did this to help keep the boys out of trouble during the Depression years. It was said that his idea was excellent as the lads of the neighbourhood were too industrious to have any time to get into any sort of trouble.

Neddy Vincent's forge, located on Donnelly's Lane, was torn down about 20 years ago. A service station was later built on the site. Vincent was an ardent horseman and used to drive pac-ers and trotters at the old Bella Vista fairgrounds at the junction of Logy Bay and Torbay Roads. Many a close race was run between Vincent and Judge on that three-quarter-mile circuit.

Vincent shod nearly all the race horses in St. John's from 1930 to 1940. Racing, other than the St. Patrick's Day events, was run off on the icy surface of Quidi Vidi Lake and was dormant until the St. John's Trotting Club revived the sport in the late 1950s.

Downton's Forge, which is now closed down, was com-pletely enclosed by private properties. The only way into the forge was by entry through the old Downton home, a middle house in a range of houses on Fleming Street. Downton learned his trade at Carnell's Carriage Factory which was located at the corner of Duckworth and Cochrane Streets. He opened his own forge in 1931 and when he died the business was closed down.

Mike Tobin operated the first tire-vulcanizing garage in Newfoundland in 1923. His garage was located on Barnes Road.

Mr. Tobin learned his trade in Minneapolis in 1920. He worked for a period with the Goodrich Rubber Co. at Akron, Ohio, before returning to St. John's to open his vulcanizing garage in Georgestown.

Like a good many other enterprising men of that era, Mr. Tobin was far ahead of his day to make his trade a paying business of that time.

Mr. Lindsay opened an upholstery shop in Davey's Lane, off Hayward Avenue. He was a master cabinet maker as well as an upholsterer. He could copy any product of the great cabinet makers of the world. Many homes in St. John's have copies of the world's great cabinet makers that were made by Lindsay.

Georgestown was well supplied with some of the best carpenters that plied their trade in St. John's.

John Davey had a large premises just off Hayward Avenue. He had shops and sheds to fabricate windows and doors. His benchmen could make a stair run and take it to a house site and there place it in the right position with only minor adjustments. His sheds contained all types of planks and wood goods used in the trade. His plans room was the heart of his operation, for it was from there that his shop crew did most of their layouts for the special items for the houses his firm built or repaired.

There were other fine, first-class carpenters, amongst whom Mr. Wiseman, Mr. Coaker and Mr. Bulger were the most notable, for all three were as much in demand as was the firm of John Davey and Co.

In the year 1862, Neil McDougald leased land from Jabez Nurse on a 30-year term at 15 pounds, ten shillings a year. The land fronted on both Barnes Road and McDougall Street. Mr. McDougald built a house and factory on the site. His house and office were entered from McDougall Street and the factory entrance was from Barnes Road. The house and office building had a slate roof. In his factory he manufactured candles, soap and oil skins. When Jabez Nurse died, most of his estate was sold at public auction. McDougald was then able to buy out the land on which he built his house and factory. However, during the time of the negotiations of purchase, McDougald died, and his son proceeded with the business, which lasted into the early 1900s.

In about the year 1924, a Mr. Jimmy Johnston purchased the house and office part of the premises and turned it into a duplex building. He lived in the east section for a few years and then moved out. The eastern unit was recently purchased by a Mr. Smythe. When he was having some major repairs made to the building, his workmen uncovered a slate-shingled portion of the roof which was in perfect condition. Due to much deterioration, he had to rebuild the roof and the slates were removed. He has, however kept them and plans to use them in some way, either on or around the house.

*

Thompson's Oil Clothing Factory was located at the rear of his residence on Georgestown Road (now Monkstown Road). The factory was serviced through a loading door fronting on William Street. In those days the fishing industry, with its allied trades, was a big employer. The supply of wet-wear (oil skins) was an essential commodity for both the fishermen and "on shore" workers connected with the harvest from the sea. Thompson's factory employed 22 people in the fabrication of oil clothes, and he supplied the fishing firms with an immediate and excellent product.

Thompson's Cottage was, at one time, the residence of William Carson. Dr. Carson was the father of Responsible Government for Newfoundland.

When Thompson died the property passed on to the Lawson family. (Mrs. Lawson was the daughter of Thompson.) Mr. Caule purchased the property in the mid-1950s, tore down the old unused buildings and residence, and replaced it with a modern house.

On the east side of Monkstown Road, approximately opposite William Street, there is a "dead end" lane called Monks Lane. Here was located the Lime Kilns of the firm of J.M. Brine, importer of the lime from Plymouth, England, and from Cork and Waterford, Ireland. The lime was used in masonry and plaster work.

Brine made lime from limestone in his kilns. The limestone was found in Newfoundland and transported to St. John's. There was a local kind of limestone that was also "burnt" in Brine's kilns. Brine manufactured a brick using clay from Pelley's Island, but he imported a fireplace brick, tiles and polished brick that were more widely used in the masonry trade that formed the bulk of his business.

When Fleming Street was realigned under a Georgestown NIP contract, recently, some old houses and fireplace foundations were excavated by the workforce. The rubble was deposited in the city dump at Robin Hood Bay before anyone with a knowledge of historical artifacts knew about it. The relics were believed to have been along Willow Street of the original Georgestown village. The bricks may have been made at Brine's Monks Lane kiln.

The Coughlan family was the courier of the Royal Mail in St. John's and surrounding area for more than 100 years. William Coughlan and his sons transported the Royal Mail along the Southern Shore, St. John's West and St. John's East Extern Districts. In early times the mail was transported in horse-drawn carriages. The mail went through in all kinds of weather, and the

Coughlan family never failed to carry out their agreements with the Newfoundland Post Office. The Coughlan stables were located on Belvedere Street and were adjacent to the old city stables that fronted on Hayward Avenue.

With the coming of the motorized age, Coughlan was quick to adapt to the new apparatus of transport, and he purchased only the best of stake body vehicles. Later, when the van-type trucks came on the market, he added one or more to his fleet. Mr. Coughlan and his sons kept their equipment in top condition and always replaced their vehicles every two years. When the senior Coughlan died, his sons continued the contract for the transport of the Royal Mail in the same efficient manner. John Coughlan was the last of the family to operate the Royal Mail contract. Today, Miss Alice Coughlan, who resides on Barnes Road, is the only member of the family in Georgestown. The Coughlan name was a household word, sort of a landmark, in the Barnes Road-Belvedere Street area for more than 100 years.

Newfoundland's foremost builder and architect family, the Southcott's—John and Tom—lived on Monkstown Road. They purchased the old Clancey estate and thereon erected some of city's finest houses. The two brothers built a fine mansion on Quigley's Lane, near Long Pond. The lane was later named Strawberry Marsh Road. The Southcott's lived there and about 50 years ago it became the Church of England Girls Orphanage. The Southcott's built a fine range of houses on Hayward Avenue and another range of three units on Monkstown Road. Both ranges of houses are still in near-perfect condition today.

Mary Southcott, daughter of John and Pamela, went to England to train as a nurse in the year 1898. She returned to St. John's in the year 1902 to become Nursing Superintendent at the General Hospital in charge of the female staff. The following year she opened the hospital's school of nursing. In the year 1914 she resigned her position at the General and opened a private hospital on Monkstown Road in a house her father and uncle had built. Her elderly parents moved into the private hospital shortly afterwards. Nurse Southcott died in the year 1943. The skyscraper Nurses Residence of the General Hospital on Forest Road is called Southcott Hall as a tribute to her work as a pioneer nurse.

Neary's Bacon and Ham Processing House was in full operation from 1909 to 1934. Mr. Neary saw the possibility of such an operation for St. John's in particular, and Newfoundland in general. His "Smoke house" and processing plant was located at the rear of his residence on Circular Road. The product, cured, processed and packaged, had a city-wide distribution and sales were always brisk. His out-of-town trade required a full-time business clerk to handle the huge volume of repeat orders for his excellent product.

Today, the only remaining building of Neary's processing plant is the old concrete smoke house. It stands like a monument to a once-prosperous industry that in all probability was the first family-owned and -operated food processing business of its kind in St. John's.

In the year 1930, an establishment known as the St. John's Co-operative Society operated a co-op general and grocery store on Mullock Street. The business was quite successful, and many of the Georgestown residents joined the ranks of the Society because of the excellent prices and top-quality provisions and goods sold by the establishment.

Many Georgestown residents were also members in the Land Development Association (A group of people who grew vegetables on lands lent to the association for the express purpose of helping to defray the cost of farm produce for families hit by the Great Depression of 1929-1933). As these families worked hard on their plots, the crop was great, and much excess vegetables resulted from their toil. The manager of the co-op store purchased this excess of produce and sold it at near cost to the society members and needy of the area, many of whom were in dire straits. The co-op store moved out of Georgestown in or about the year 1945.

The Newfoundland Brewery Co. was first opened on April 13, 1893, but on February 11, 1894, the new establishment burnt to the ground. A general meeting of the shareholders was called within two weeks to decide on a course of action. At this time Mr. J.V. O'Dea was the secretary of the Newfoundland Brewery Co. and a substantial shareholder. Some of the original shareholders sold their holdings but most stayed and decided to rebuild on the burnt-out site. The new building was started in mid-May and the Brewery was in full production by October 1, 1895. It was in this year that the O'Dea family became the principal shareholders, and eventually the controllers of the Newfoundland Brewery.

In the year 1940, Mr. J.R. O'Dea, who was now the managing director, renovated the Brewery on modern lines and in a fireproof building. In early 1961, the Newfoundland Brewery Ltd. was sold to Molson Ltd. of Montreal and is now operated by that company.

The late Senator J.G. Higgins Q.C. operated a modern weather station from his home in the year 1926. Higgins resided at 31 Monkstown Road. The house is the first in a range of three, which was built by Southcott's in or about the year 1883. This range of houses is on Monkstown Road and south of William Street. Mr. Higgins had his wind-velocity and directional-apparatus atop his home. It was as good as a time piece to the residents of the area, for every morning at about 7:00 A.M. the gentleman would climb through a roof hatch to record the direction and speed of the wind no matter the condition of the weather.

The range-measuring devices and temperature gauges or glasses were housed in the standard latticed, white-coloured boxes and located in his backyard. His barometers were positioned in the roof-covered verandah at the back of the house.

Mr. Higgins reported his data on the weather twice daily to the radio stations call numbers V.O.G.Y. and V.O.N.F. and they, in turn, broadcast the information to the radio-listening public on the hour every hour as their up-to-date weather-and-forecast report.

Georgestown had three taxi stands within its boundaries. Rawlins Cross Taxi was started in or about 1926 by a man named Willy Joe Martin. At first, he operated singly until 1929-30. The taxi service was generally known as "Martin's—I'm Alone Taxi." In that year a Mr. Murrin became a partner and the business became "Rawlins Cross Taxi Service." A Mr. Billy King entered the business in June 1936, giving the service a third car. The following year each partner added a new sedan to the fleet and it stayed at a six-car taxi service for the next five years. Due to the problems of supply in new car manufactures during the war (World War II), the service was reduced to a full-time taxi service for three cars. One car was scrapped for replacement parts and tires and two were kept in reserve as backup vehicles. The Rawlins Cross Taxi Stand was located at the junction of Monkstown and Rennie's Mill River Roads.

Mr. Martin died in the year 1948, but Mr. Murrin and Mr. King kept the service going until late in the year 1961, when the city decided to redesign the busy intersection. The roads were widened, islands were installed where the offices of the taxi stand were located, and a series of one-way traffic lanes were laid in. Where once a small, but active, business was thriving, only a grassy island stands in the middle of a constant flow of one-way traffic today.

7 Monkstown Road
Possibly built for Sir Hugh Hoyles between 1865 and 1875. Over the years, the building has been home to Sir Hugh Hoyles, Prime Minister and Chief Justice, John Stewart Currie, publisher of the *Daily News*, and author Margaret Duley. The building retains its original slate roof and many of its interior and exterior architectural details. It was designated as a municipal heritage building by the City of St. John's in September 2002. (Courtesy of the Heritage Society of Newfoundland and Labrador)

The 4158 Taxi Stand was owned by Mr. Joe Mulrooney. He began his business at the corner of Fleming Street and Donnelly's Lane where E.O'D. Kelly started his automobile distributorship in the year 1937. Two years later Mr. Mulrooney purchased two new vehicles from the firm of Terra Nova Motors Ltd. They were then the Newfoundland distributors for Nash Motors Ltd. They delivered the Ambassador models to Mr. Mulrooney in the month of September. He had the cars equipped with radio communication by Marconi Ltd. His drivers were always in touch with the office. When one fare was taken to its destination, the driver was given another fare by radio contact and in this manner the 4158 Taxi Service cut down on wear and tear and fuel consumption due mainly to the radio communication system that Mr. Mulrooney had the foresight to install in his vehicles in 1939.

The 4158 Taxi Service was closed out in 1960 due to the health of its proprietor. However, Mr. Mulrooney, as mentioned previously, is today the bursar at Brother Rice Monastery on Bonaventure Avenue.

Mr. Bert Trask opened a taxi stand and service station in his new building at the corner of Empire Avenue and Allandale Road shortly after his return from overseas. He was on duty with the Royal Canadian Air Force 1941-1945, where he rose to the rank of Flight Sergeant.

He ran a fine and efficient taxi and service station business for more than ten years. In the year 1956, he sold his building and closed out both the taxi stand and service station (Mr. Jim Smith opened a body shop at that place shortly after he purchased the building from Trask).

Mr. Trask opened a used car sales business on Topsail Road which he operated with great success until 1976, when he closed down and moved to Vancouver, where he now resides in retirement.

Mr. Fred Lindsay opened his furniture repair and upholstery shop in Davey's Lane off Hayward Avenue, in the year
1916. Although Lindsay's business was the repair and upholstery
of furniture, it was said of him that he could duplicate any piece
of furniture originally made by the great masters of the past such
as Hipplewaite, Sheridan, Chipendale and others. Some of these
copies made by Lindsay adorn the living rooms of the older
homes of St. John's today. His copies of the Queen Anne and
Victoria era of furniture appeared to be the favourites of the buying public in his day.

George Davey and Company, Builders and Contractors
were one of the biggest firms in the construction of homes in the
first half of the century. John Davey lived at 19 Maxse Street,
while his brothers and uncle lived outside the boundaries of
Georgestown. Their shops were in Davey's Lane, off Hayward
Avenue.

The main shed housed the office and bench workshops.
(Bench workshops were where the final parts of external fixtures
such as stair runs, door facings and such trim work were made
before being brought out and installed in the houses that were
almost complete.) The other sheds were used for the storage of
lumber and work tools such as ladders and scaffolding. Two
other buildings in the Davey compound were hired out. One
housed Fred Lindsay's Furniture and Upholstery Shop. When
Davey's was closed out several years ago, the buildings rapidly
deteriorated, and when the property was sold, the new owner
tore down the old sheds. Today the area that once housed a great
industry of the carpentry trade is known as Davey's Field.

John Warren, who owned and operated a hardware store
on Water Street in the early decades of the twentieth century, was
a master craftsman. His hobby was the making of useful articles
requiring great skill of hands to assemble the complex and intri-

cate parts into a workable model. On several occasions he manu-factured hand-operated looms for the weaving of wool into cloth. His son, Francis, learned similar skills and today is an expert on the cutting and setting of local precious stones. His favourite gemstone is Labradorite and his jewellery creations with this stone are highly sought by collectors and the general public. Mr. F. Warren resides at 12 Bonaventure Avenue.

Of all the old contracting-and-building firms that grew up in the Georgestown area of St. John's, only Henry J. Thomas and Sons Ltd. is still in business today. The firm started in 1857 and has steadily grown through the years.

In all probability their most famous contract was that awarded the firm in the year 1898. The previous year on September 22, 1897, Newfoundland's first Roman Catholic Archbishop, the Most Rev. Michael Francis Howley, laid the cor-nerstone for Cabot Tower, on Signal Hill. Henry J. Thomas and Sons finished the now-famous landmark by late October 1899. The tower was officially opened September 20, 1900. Henry J. Thomas and Sons Ltd. started up business on Barnes Road, but today has premises that extend out to Catherine Street. Approximately 12 years ago they purchased the property that in earlier times was Fred J. Dodd's Central Garage. The rights to Gorman's Lane were earlier acquired from City Council, so today that laneway is fenced off. The old Dunne Cottage had been pur-chased in or about the year 1946. The Thomas building and con-struction firm contains about one acre of valuable property in the city.

James Dunne opened up a furniture moving business in 1887. At that time all his mode of transport was horse-drawn equipment. Dunne's was the most reliable company for moving pianos or organs in St. John's. Nearly all the furniture-manufac-turers and importers like Callahan and Glass Co. used Dunne's services. With the coming of the motor age to St. John's, Dunne adapted his methods accordingly. Mr. Dunne lived on Barnes Road. His grandson, James Dunne, who lives on Hayward Avenue, carries on the business today.

Georgestown has had many talented residents in all avenues down through the years; but none were more gifted than Leo Dillon. Leo was the second child of Richard and Mary Dillon who resided at 3 Hayward Avenue. He was born September 23, 1896. In his formative years, Leo attended St. Patrick's Hall School. In his third year at school, the boy entered the Junior Choir. The choirmaster (a Christian Brother) soon learned that young Dillon was gifted with an extraordinary soprano voice and he spent much time teaching Dillon to sing arias from operas and popular classical songs. This training continued for several years and when Leo Dillon was 11, he was elevated to the school's Senior Choir.

In July of 1907, the choirmaster went to Ireland on holiday and to visit his family after more than ten years in St. John's. The Christian Brother (choirmaster) was returning to St. John's in August when he met up with a fellow passenger who was also coming out to St. John's. This man was a professor of music and was making his first trip to St. John's. His name was William Moncrieff Mawer. During one of their shipboard conversations, the young professor mentioned that he specialized in voice but was capable of teaching all forms of musical instruments.

When the ship docked in St. John's the two men went their different ways but agreed to keep in touch with one another. School reopened September 3, 1907 and the usual activities were once more the way of life for both student and teacher.

The Christian Brothers Schools were all preparing musical productions for a big event: the Superior General of the Order was to visit St. John's, and each school was to stage a production of either a play or a musical in honour of the visit.

The Brother (choirmaster) in charge of St. Patrick's School Choir knew that young Dillon would be capable of lead singing roles even though he was one of the youngest boys in the choir. Practices were held daily and all was going well with the choral work for the operetta "Iolanthe."

It was now early October, but the acting roles were not going very well. The Brother remembered Professor Mawer and asked him to visit his choir practice. The Professor came and conducted the practice. However, he detected a sour voice in the choir. He had the group sing a second time with hopes of locating the "broken voice." This method failed, so he lined up the boys and had each lad go on stage and sing a verse or few lines solo. If the voice was good, he would say, "You are all right. Next lad up." When it came to young Dillon's turn, the Professor looked up. He said, "Repeat that song in this key." He did this several times until he reached the highest note, then he said, "Boys you may all leave, but you young lad, stay." The Professor had young Dillon sing the aria over a few more times. He then called the boy to him and gave him a note. He told him to go down to Hutton's Music Store, ask for the musical score that was written on the note and take it home, where he was to study and practice the words. He told him to know it by the middle of the following week when he would be back to conduct the singing of the scores.

When the week had passed, the Professor was true to his word. He had the lad sing while he played the music. Dillon was able to sing the entire song without error. The songs contained the highest notes in the scale. The Professor told the choirmaster that he would have to rearrange the cast for young Dillon was indeed the most talented voice he had ever heard. He told the

Brother to give the boy the lead role so that all may hear what a young boy's voice could do in song.

The following year, William Moncrieff Mawer was appointed organist at St. Andrew's Presbyterian Church, a position he held until 1912. The Professor left St. John's and sailed to New York. He had, however, given young Dillon several lessons over the years and even asked the boy's parents to let him go along with him where he could get better training and was sure to succeed in opera. The Professor returned to St. John's and was again organist at St. Andrew's from 1920 to 1924. Professor Mawer had such successful St. John's pianists as Bob McLeod and the late Ian Cowan as pupils who also became organists at St. Andrew's.

Leo Dillon was one of the city's best tenors and was always in demand by all associations and groups who staged concerts and musical plays.

In 1931, the Benevolent Irish Society's St. Patrick's Day Parade was cancelled because of the *Viking* disaster, but the annual St. Patrick's Day concerts were staged both in the afternoon and at night. That night, Leo Dillon performed on stage at the Casino. It was said that his rendition of the "Londonderry Air" was so good that everyone in the theatre knew that his voice was at its best and that it was sung for a life-long friend who died in the ill-fated *Viking* at the ice fields.

Dillon never sang songs unless they were arias from operas or musicals. He sang Irish songs written by the best Irish composers and Scottish airs were his favourites.

In 1932, Dillon was singing at a nearby town in mid-winter. After the concert the party left the hall in the height of a snowstorm. He and a fellow singer started to walk after their car had gotten bogged down. They reached safety in a house almost a mile from their car. Dillon contracted pneumonia and it is said that it affected his golden voice. He did sing for many years after, but his days as a concert performer were to end in 1940. Leo died in 1961. His son Patrick and some of his grandchildren reside in Georgestown.

VII

Michael Kearney: Newfoundland's Greatest Shipbuilder

In the morning papers, dated March 5, 1885, there appeared the death notice of Michael Kearney, resident of James (now Mullock) Street in Georgestown. The notice stated that Mr. Kearney passed peacefully away in the forenoon of March 4, 1885. His age was given as 76 years.

Michael Kearney, shipbuilder, was born at Ferryland in the year 1809. He was descended from one of the oldest Irish families in Newfoundland. It has been stated that his great, great, grandfather came out to Ferryland with Sir George Calvert's (later Lord Baltimore) first colonists to settle the province of Avalon, the territory granted to him in letters patent by James I of Great Britain. When Baltimore's Colony failed and the nobleman moved to the then American Colonies, many of the early colonists (including Kearney's great, great, grandfather) remained in Ferryland. Here they fished, farmed and cut timber in the forests. Some stayed in Ferryland, but over the years most moved into St. John's or to small settlements along the Southern Shore.

At an early age, Kearney became keenly interested in shipbuilding, sailmaking, cargo space, passenger accommodations and the related necessities, such as an abundant supply of fresh water and the disposal of liquid-and-solid wastes in sea-going vessels. In about the year 1825, he went to sea as a seaman on an ocean-going ship in order to learn more about the workings of vessels' construction. He spent the next two years on ships in the foreign-going trade of Newfoundland. Then in the early summer of 1827, Michael Kearney sailed to Waterford, Ireland where he apprenticed to a shipbuilding company in that city. Young Kearney adapted to the work with a grim determination to learn every phase of the art of shipbuilding from designs, layouts and finally the construction of the designed vessels. His determination was well rewarded, for within three years he had completed his tenure of apprenticeship and was considered such a professional shipbuilder by his employer that he was given a position of superintendent in charge of the construction of wooden vessels up to 350 tons draft.

Kearney stayed with the Waterford Shipbuilding Company for the next four or five years. He gained valuable experience in all the known methods of wooden ships construction. His work was of such a high quality that he received many offers from shipbuilding companies in Ireland and England. However, in the spring of 1834, Kearney left the Waterford Shipbuilding Company and moved to the town of Youghal in South Waterford County, where he spent the next two years with a small boat-building firm. His move to the shipyard was done in order that he might learn their methods of construction of skiff-type open boats.

Even at this late date his mind was set on returning to Newfoundland where he would set up his own shipyards and construct vessels from Newfoundland timber. He returned to Ferryland in the summer of 1838. In that year he began building "inshore" open boats. He moved to St. John's in the month of

February 1840 and set up the Kearney Shipyards on the south side of the harbour where he immediately set to work building his first brig, the *Mary Hounsell*, a ship of 300 tons that was launched in the spring of the year 1842. The *Mary Hounsell* was built for a Mr. Daniel Fowler of St. John's. The event was of such great importance that the governor of the day, Sir John Harvey, sent letters of congratulations to both the owner and the builder of the vessel.

Kearney not only built boats in his own shipyards, but moved around the island of Newfoundland plying his skills for those who hired him. In the year 1843, Michael Kearney built the brig *Saint Fillian* at Spaniard's Bay for a Mr. Donnelly, a very wealthy merchant of that town. This vessel was later purchased by a St. John's mercantile firm who used her as a foreign-going freighter. Another boat, the barque *Thomas Ridley* was built at Carbonear for a merchant named Rourke, in the year 1852. The *Thomas Ridley* was a boat of 170 tons, gross, draft, and it is said to have been the biggest sealing vessel working out of a Newfoundland port at that time. This boat is known to have sailed from Cape St. Francis, Newfoundland, to Cape Clare, Ireland, in nine days, an impressive accomplishment for crossing the Atlantic under sail by any standards.

Among the many ships that Kearney built, perhaps the clipper barque *Rothesay* (also built in the year 1852), of 200 tons, gross, was his fastest sailer. The *Rothesay*, built at the Victoria Street dockyard, could outsail all ships that she came in contact with on the high seas. On one occasion she was known to have beaten the clipper barque *Tasso* on a run from Pernambuco (now Recife), Brazil to St. John's by a full day.

The prettiest boat to have been built by Kearney was, in all probability, the *Gauntlett*, a yacht made to order for Baine Johnston Co. of St. John's, and built in the Kearney Shipyard in

the year 1843. It is said that this yacht was built for the sole purpose of sailing to the Cocos Islands in quest of the famed treas-
ure on the islands. In the course of her voyage to the islands, the
Gauntlett was given chase by a pirate ship. After skilful manoeu-
vring, the trim little yacht easily outsailed the Caribbean corsair.
The *Gauntlett* was later given the Royal Yacht Pennant to fly in
England as she had no equal there as a sailer.

In the year 1855, Kearney built the brigantine *Ida* for the
Hon. C.F. Bennett. This boat was built in Bennett's Boatyard, then
situated where the General Post Office is presently located on
Water Street. When the vessel was completed, it was launched by
crossing Water Street and going down Bennett's Cove Lane into
the harbour. The lane was so narrow that Mr. Bennett became
worried for fear that his new vessel would get stuck between the
buildings on both sides of the laneway.

Mr. Kearney assured him that he had nothing to worry
about. Taking a hammer from one of the workmen, Kearney
drove a nail into the mortar between brickwork in the wall and
hung his gold watch on it. Turning to Mr. Bennett he wagered
both the watch and its value in coin that the boat would not touch
it as it slid through on its way to the waters of the harbour. The
Ida was launched without incident much to the relief of Mr.
Bennett. Kearney took his watch off the nail and placed it in his
pocket. The *Ida* was the fastest vessel in her class sailing out of
London, England in the second half of the 1850s. On one occasion
she sailed from St. John's to Bristol, England in the time of 13
days and made the return trip in exactly the same time. The *Ida*
was commanded by Captain J. Callahan of St. John's. Other
famous ships built in the Kearney Shipyards in St. John's were
the *Arrabella Tarbot, Naomi* and *Three Sisters*, all for the famous
Captain Munden of Brigus. Kearney built so many ships that the
exact total is unknown.

Michael Kearney married Bridget Blackler of Tors Cove in the district of Ferryland, in the year 1839. He took up residence in a cottage on Georgestown (now Monkstown) Road which he leased from a Mr. Jabez Nurse. It was in this cottage that Mr. Kearney drew up most of his ships' designs and negotiated the agreements with the parties for whom the vessels were built. Kearney moved to James (now Mullock) Street in or about the year 1848, when he purchased a house on that street. This house became his permanent residence and it was from here that he carried on his social life up to the time of his death on March 4, 1885. The old cottage on Georgestown (now Monkstown) Road became the property of Jabez N. Finlay (a grandson of Jabez Nurse) now in occupancy of a Mr. Newell. It was later purchased by a Michael B. Kearney, city accountant in the year 1888 who was a nephew of Michael Kearney, the great shipbuilder.

When Michael Kearney set up his shipbuilding yard at St. John's South Side in the year 1840, by his skill and unceasing efforts, he established and promoted an industry in Newfoundland which greatly reduced the necessity of vessel importation from the New England States, England and the Maritime Colonies. Local merchants and outport planters soon found that the local-built vessels were larger, stronger and more suitable to the coastal waters of Newfoundland. This industry also began a cycle of changes in St. John's, the main being an abrupt end to a large portion of seasonal employment.

Michael Kearney was a man of great skill and ingenuity, the pioneer builder of the Newfoundland sailing fleet and the craftsman who built the vessels on which Newfoundland's great sea captains and skippers incessantly battled the forces of nature in her worst moods, helping to make this country's glorious marine history. He died at St. John's on March 4, 1885.

Such great mariners as the Jackmans, Winsors, Bartletts, Keans, Mundens and Blandfords, to name but a few, cannot be equalled for bravery, daring and complete seamanship.

The advent of the steam-driven vessels greatly reduced the large square-rigged sailing ships and local merchants sailed with the times. With this change, the local shipbuilding industry faded and St. John's adjusted its craftsmen in due course of time. Had Michael Kearney been living at the time of revolution, it is reasonable to assume that he would have had foresight enough to meet the challenge. Had we been fortunate enough to have men of his ability amongst us in the early years of change from wood to steel, it is possible that Newfoundland would have become the world's foremost maritime nation and St. John's the maritime capital.

VIII

The Avalon Athletic Club

Sporting events in old St. John's date back to the late decades of the 1700s. Team games such as cricket (which it is believed was first played in St. John's between 1680-90), rowing races and tug o' war were usually conducted between soldiers of the garrisons and sailors of the numerous ships of the Royal Navy that were stationed in St. John's. Running races, swimming races and walking matches were always events that drew many spectators. Tug o' war contests were common events, for whenever a Royal Navy ship entered port, its crew would challenge the best team of the day for a match. The contest would take place somewhere along the waterfront or on the parade grounds of one of the garrisons in St. John's.

Horse racing and cockfighting matches were weekly events during the summer months dating back to 1807. These events were known as "money matches" because high monetary stakes were wagered on the outcome of the contests. Purses as high as 500 pounds sterling were won in some of the horse races. A challenge race between horses owned by Doctors Carson and Kielley in the year 1818 for a purse of 200 pounds sterling was the most famous contest of that year. It was said that because of the political rivalry between the two gentlemen, large amounts in side betting were placed on the outcome of this race by the supporters of the opposing political views. The St. John's Races were the major horse racing contests of the racing season. These were usually held in mid-September and were run over the best courses available. The race courses at Casey's Estate and at Best's Farm were usually the sites for the St. John's Races. Quidi Vidi Lake was always the site for wintertime horse racing contests. All racing events were run over measured courses and the official judge's rulings were always accepted as final.

Cockfighting matches were held outside the confines of the old St. John's. This sport is believed to have been brought into St. John's from the American colonies. The first known cockfight was reported to have taken place about the year 1807 and the prize to the winner valued at 25 pounds sterling. The clergy were against this form of sport and the betting that accompanied the matches. They spoke regularly of the widespread gambling from their pulpits at Sunday services. Many farms in the outlying region of the city had "cockpits" which were hidden from public view. In these fighting arenas for birds, much gambling did take place. The most famous site was supposed to be in the vicinity of present-day Craigmillar Avenue. This avenue was originally known as Cockpit Road and somewhere along that public way, the sport had its most popular cockpit. The constant preachings by the clergy finally prevailed and the sport faded away.

Winter sporting events such as speed skating, curling matches and shinny (the early form of hockey) all took place on the frozen ice surface of Quidi Vidi Lake. Some minor skating races were run off on Upper and Middle Long Ponds. However, the big speed skating competitions, which were very popular, took place on Quidi Vidi Lake from about 1830 to 1857. After that date most meets were held in many of the skating rinks that sprung up all over old St. John's. The last of the indoor skating rinks fell victims to the Great Fire of 1892, and then Quidi Vidi Lake became the competition arena once more.

Curling games were played on Quidi Vidi Lake in the area near the present-day site of the boat house. The club executives hired a man who lived near lakeside to clean off the ice surface when snowstorms and snowdrifts filled in the curling lanes. The caretaker also kept the temporary rooms (portable sheds) clean, neat and tidy all season. He had to provide firewood to heat the rooms for the comfort and convenience of the club members. The main shed held a small canteen where refreshments and hot drinks could be obtained while the late evening games were in progress.

It was said that on one occasion, a big snowstorm broke on St. John's early in the day that the championship match (draw) was to take place. The caretaker erected a temporary, high snow fence, made from spruce "longers" and well cross-braced. The framework, which was erected the length of the rink along the west snow wall, was covered with old sail can-vass. This "snow fence" collected the drifting snow and formed a wind break. The storm abated about 4:00 P.M. and the caretak-er, with the help of his family, swept the ice clean. At 7:00 P.M. the teams took to the curling lanes and a champion was decided that night. The game of curling was introduced to old St. John's in or about the year 1838. It was an outdoor sport until the Avalon Club built a curling rink around 1871. From that, the "roaring game" moved indoors and seldom, if ever, was played outside on Quidi Vidi Lake as other suitable works were built in the city.

Football, cricket and tennis flourished in St. John's at the turn of the century (1900) and each sport had its loyal followers. Cricket soon began to decline, and by the year 1923, this team game was gone. Football and tennis are still actively supported by both players and fans.

Athletic activities of an indoor nature got a firm foundation in St. John's in the year 1898 when the Reid family began the construction of the Prince's Rink on Factory Lane in the Hoylestown area of the city. The rink was officially opened in January 1899. In February the first hockey match was played on its ice surface between a visiting Canadian team from Nova Scotia and a city team made up of the best players from the local clubs.

The Reids built the rink to provide recreation for their employees, the engineers, architects, clerks, accountants, machinists and other essential personnel who came from Canada to build the Reid Newfoundland Railway. The rink, however, was open to all and associations of St. John's soon entered into the City Hockey League which was formed within the next year. The famous Boyle Trophy was donated by Sir Cavendish Boyle, the then Governor of Newfoundland, in the year 1903 and it became the emblem of supremacy in the City Hockey League. (A book titled *We Love Thee Newfoundland*, written by Frank W. Graham, gives the entire history of Gov. Cavendish Boyle and of the historic trophy he donated to the City Hockey League.)

Within the next decade, indoor sports became very popular and many clubs were formed throughout the city. In 1908 the Avalon Athletic Club was formed to promote the sport of wrestling in St. John's. An old schoolhouse on Fleming Street in the Georgestown area of the city was obtained and used as the club's home. The school was formerly known as "Hannah Barnes's School" and closed down when Miss Barnes married J.B. Mitchell.

The wrestling form instructed in the club was styled along the lines of the Olympic Roman-Greco rules. The charter members had among their number a Fred Marshall who was the outstanding St. John's athlete of his time. Marshall was the premier miler of Newfoundland having covered the mile course in four minutes, 50 seconds in an official track meet held on August 16, 1911. The mark stood up for more than 20 years before it was beaten in the 1930s.

Executive directors of the club were Wm. O'D. Kelly, Ern Goodland, Mr. B. Mitchell and Reg Dowden. The athlete members were George Marshall, Harry Duff, Bob Reid, Stan Cullen, Jack Campbell, Otto Oppelt, Ed. Barnes, George Knight, Alex Hennebury, Ewen Hennebury, Fred Marshall and Young Olsen. Junior members (schoolboys) were Peter Cook, Norm Halfyard, Freddy Noseworthy, Gord Taylor, Max Churchill, Alex Kelly, William Adams and Edmund Kelly. Otto Oppelt left the club and in the following year formed a similar athletic club in the West End.

The Avalon Athletic Club on Fleming Street was the site of the first wrestling matches in St. John's. After a year of training instructions in the art of wrestling under the capable direction and coaching of Young Olsen, who was the club's physical instructor and wrestling tutor, a card of wrestling bouts was presented to the public on the night of September 17, 1909:

FRED MARSHALL

VS

ALEX HENNEBURY

(WON BY FRED MARSHALL)

STAN CULLEN

VS

JACK CAMPBELL

(WON BY STAN CULLEN)

EWAN HENNEBURY

VS

GEORGE MARSHALL

(WON BY EWAN HENNEBURY)

REFEREES: ERN GOODLAND, REG DOWDEN AND YOUNG OLSEN.

Olsen gave a demonstration of wrestling holds to the audience at the end of the main events. Fred Marshall, Stan Cullen, Alex Hennebury, George Marshall and Jack Campbell took part in the demonstration.

Wrestling bouts were held every weekend at the Fleming Street club and were always well attended by the sporting public. Fred Marshall was considered the best local wrestler and Stan Cullen was a close second. Marshall was quick and strong and had the ability to outmanoeuvre his opponents with a masterful ease. Cullen was slighter, but as agile as a cat. He had great strength of hands, but was not as strong as Marshall. Whenever the two were scheduled to wrestle any opponent, the house was full. When Cullen and Marshall tangled on the mat, it was standing room only with a 300-foot-long lineup outside on the street.

The Hennebury brothers, Alex and Ewan, were also great crowd pleasers and Jack Campbell was not far behind with his style of wrestling. However, Fred Marshall, Stan Cullen and the Hennebury brothers usually represented the Avalon Athletic

Club in citywide competitions that were held at the Prince's Rink or C.L.B. Armoury.

Young Olsen, the club's physical instructor and wrestling coach, fought Stan Anderson of Canada, the then world light-weight wrestling champion, in the C.L.B. on the night of November 20, 1911. Olsen won the match and title by two falls to one in the elapsed time of 65 minutes. About six months later Olsen successfully defended his title when he again defeated Anderson in two straight falls. Elapsed time was less than 18 minutes. The victory was so swift and so decisive that the fans were said to have called the match "only a warm-up session for our champ."

Young Olsen won many matches in both the Prince's Rink and C.L.B., but they were minor events compared to his title bouts with Sam Anderson. In 1913, Olsen left St. John's and went to the United States to take a wrestling coach position with a university in the Boston, Massachusetts area. He married Irene Dechest, the daughter of a prominent Harrisonburg, Virginia lawyer. Olsen moved to Harrisonburg, where he took a position as physical instructor at the public school. He retired from wrestling and devoted all of his time to physical instruction at the school.

The Avalon Athletic Club died out when war broke out in 1914. Many of the athletes went overseas with the Royal Newfoundland Regiment. Most of them excelled in other branches of athletic abilities in St. John's from 1908-1914.

Fred Marshall was the outstanding athletic figure of the era. He was the best middle distance and mile runner as well as a standout in his position on the football pitch. He competed in the marathon every year and always placed near the top on every occasion. He was a strong swimmer and, although not the winner, he was always considered a great contender in every meet.

His mile record time of four minutes, 50 seconds was established on St. George's Field in the year 1911. His nearest competition was more than 200 yards behind when Marshall crossed the finish line.

When World War I ended, Marshall competed in the Allied Games, held in Paris, as the Royal Newfoundland Regiment wrestling representative. He lost out in the finals for his weight class by a judge's decision when both men had won a fall and the final fall appeared to end in a stalemate under the time rule. When one considers the total number of contestants at that meet, Marshall's showing was, indeed, worthy of the highest praise. Marshall returned to St. John's and once more competed in track and field meets. Although not as fast as in former days, he won the mile racing event until he retired from active competition.

Stan Cullen was one of the most remarkable athletes of his time. He was a great sprinter and always did exceptionally well in every track meet he entered. He teamed up with Jack Campbell, Geo. Knight and Eric St. George to become known as the "C.C.C. Flyers" relay team. They were the greatest relay team of that decade. (The relay teams of that era were three-man competitions so one of the four had to take his turn as the substitute.) The C.C.C. Flyers were never beaten when they competed with the other brigade meets. Cullen was an excellent wrestler and rated next to Fred Marshall in that sport. In later years Stan became the best referee in St. John's for wrestling and boxing. When his days of competition ended, he conducted lessons in model building in St. John's and also gave classes in photography. Cullen was a great outdoorsman. He tried every type of sport known in his time. He was good at curling and even entered speed skating races. When the automobile came to St. John's, Cullen was one of the first to own a motorcycle. He toured nearly all of the Avalon Peninsula taking scenic photographs for use in his photography studio.

Some of the junior members (schoolboys when the Avalon Athletic Club was formed) did very well in sport and brigade activities in later years.

Peter Cook became an outstanding bugler with the C.L.B. bugle band. He was selected to play the Last Post at the Newfoundland Memorial Day (July 1) ceremonies held at our National War Memorial. Peter was a professional fireman who was killed when thrown from his seat when the horses drawing a ladder-apparatus vehicle took flight due to the backfiring of a fire engine while coming out of the old Central Fire Hall.

Alex Kelly was an excellent inter-collegiate athlete when he played on football and hockey teams and as a member of track teams while at St. Bon's. When he attended St. Francis Xavier University in Nova Scotia, he was the leading scorer on their hockey team. His brother Edmund, when he entered St. Francis Xavier three years later, also made his place on the hockey team. The following year Edmund was elected captain of the University hockey team. On returning to St. John's, Alex articled as a law student with the legal firm of Wood and Kelly. When he was admitted to the bar, he joined that firm. When Edmund returned home, he started in business and became the biggest automobile dealer in Newfoundland. He retired in 1951.

To conclude, the old schoolhouse that had become the home of the Avalon Atlantic Club fell into ruin in the early 1920s. It caught fire several times and was finally sold. The new owner subsequently tore down the ruin. The foundation was good, so three new houses were built on some of the old footings. All three houses have their main entrances on Coleman's Place (formerly Hutchings Place), but one has a side entrance fronting on Fleming Street.

IX

The General Protestant Academy

In the year 1880, Walter Grieve, John McGregor and others, as directors of the General Protestant Academy, entered into a lease with the Honourable James Tobin. The term of this lease was for a duration of 99 years. The deed of agreement contained a dwelling house and a building that was converted into a private school. At the rear of the buildings was a large field that measured more than 10,000 square feet in area. It was also included in the lease. The property fronted on Monkstown (formerly Georgestown) Road and measured 94 feet. It was bounded on the south by the property of Captain Terrance Halleran (a famous sealing skipper of that era) and on the north the boundary was property owned by James Grant. Mr. Grant was a merchant and fox farm owner. His farm was located in the Queen Victoria Hills area of St. John's. That area is more commonly known today as the "Three Pond Barrens" of which the southern slopes make up a large portion of C.A. Pippy Park and most of the area comes under the control of the Park.

The private school, known as the St. John's Academy, was instituted by John Valentine Nugent after the General Academy closed out in 1850. When the government set up its non-denominational school in 1845, Mr. Nugent was its principal. In 1860 Mr. Nugent retired and the school was closed down. When the directors of the General Protestant Academy learned of the closure, they acted quickly and took over the school. Professor Adam Scott, who was a teacher at the St. John's Academy and resided in the dwelling adjacent to the school, was installed as headmaster of the General Protestant Academy.

In order to better understand the circumstances that brought about the denominational school system, a brief summary of events concerning the Educational Act is incorporated in this chapter.

In the year 1836, the government of the day passed an educational act that did not satisfy the religious denominations. Much bickering ensued because of the many shortcomings of the Act.

In 1843 another Act that should have been an improvement on its predecessor did not accomplish much more. However, the government opened its own non-denominational academy in St. John's and the man who had been the first school inspector, Mr. J.V. Nugent, was appointed the principal when the institution opened in 1845. This school, known as the General Academy, was located near the foot of Signal Hill Road. The building selected for the school had been the residence of John Dunscombe, a wealthy merchant who, after a disastrous fire wiped out his business in the spring of 1844, left Newfoundland in the late summer of 1845. The General Academy was never accepted by the public as the citizens endorsed their church leaders' objections towards the non-denominational attitude of the government. At no time did enrolment in the academy exceed more than 18 pupils.

Bishop Fleming opposed this academy because regulations prevented him from any control in matters of religious instruction for Catholics at the institution. Bishop Feild was such an outspoken opponent of the academy that in 1844 he established the Church of England Secondary Education School for boys in a building on Forest Road. The following year he founded the Diocesan Girls School in a building near St. Thomas's Church on Military Road. Bishop Feild was determined to force the government into dividing the Protestant grant according to population as he could see that the Methodists were making inroads upon the Church of England.

It was Bishop Feild who championed the denominational system of education for Newfoundland. In this cause he was ably supported by Bishop Fleming and by the church leaders of the other faiths. This led to three changes in the Education Act in 1851, 1852 and 1853 before it became partly acceptable to the clergy. However, much bickering and friction continued as Dr. Mullock, the new Catholic bishop, strongly objected to the daily scripture readings from the Authorized Version of the Bible in Catholic schools. Bishop Feild argued the claim that "Education must have religion." This matter was foremost for many years and soon other church leaders added their support to the cause for church control of schools. In 1874, the government finally agreed to establish a straight denominational system of education under church control throughout Newfoundland.

The General Academy, which was a complete failure, was permanently closed in 1850. Mr. Nugent, its only principal, later opened a private school on Monkstown Road which was known as the St. John's Academy and became the General Protestant Academy in 1860.

The Secondary School for boys—Bishop Feild's creation in 1844—became the Church of England Academy (a name the good bishop had originally intended for his 1844 school), and rapidly increased in enrolment. The old school on Forest Road was replaced with a new building complex capable of taking "boarders" as well as day students. The new facilities erected on Bond Street also had proper accommodation for a headmaster's residence.

Bishop Mullock established St. Bonaventure's College in 1856 and the first classes were conducted in the old Palace on

Henry Street. On April 27, 1857, the bishop laid the cornerstone for St. Bon's College's first building on the site of what was formerly known as Halley's cottage grounds. That property was adjacent to the Williams Plantation that the late Bishop Fleming had obtained in 1838 and upon which he had erected his Cathedral Palace and convents with schools.

In 1886, Governor DesVoeux laid the cornerstone for the Methodist College on Long's Hill. This building with all its records and documents pertaining to its church control was destroyed in the Great Fire of 1892. It was replaced by a new brick building on the original site and was named the Wesleyan College. It was again destroyed by fire in 1925. Once more a new building arose on the same site and, like its predecessor, was renamed, this time becoming Holloway School.

The General Protestant Academy was the institute of learning mainly for the children of the adherents of the Presbyterian and Congregational faiths. The old St. John's Academy of John Nugent was a one-storey structure with a steep gabled roof. The ground floor contained the classrooms and the basement had spacious rooms for indoor activities when the weather was inclement and the playgrounds too wet for the usual activities during recess periods. The attic had accommodation for the school caretaker as well as ample space for school supplies and equipment storage. The caretaker was also the property guardian when classes closed for the day. The new directors of the academy made improvements to the building and had several extensions made at the rear of the school during the summer of 1861 so that all would be ready for the September opening of the academy. The headmaster's residence was also renovated and improved so that the directors could hold their annual meeting at the academy's headmaster's residence.

The headmaster, Adam Scott, was born in Scotland in 1823 and was a Presbyterian. It was believed that he came to St. John's to teach at the Church of England's Secondary School for boys in 1847. When the General Academy opened he was asked to join Mr. Nugent to teach at that institution. When the school failed, he moved with Mr. Nugent to the St. John's Academy and when Mr. Nugent closed down that school, Scott was asked to take the headmaster's position at the General Protestant Academy.

Professor Scott ran the academy along the lines of a British Public School and filled his staff with qualified teachers, most of whom came from Scotland and England. Scott's family of two sons and three daughters were all born in St. John's and all attended classes at the academy. In 1877, Scott, who was a frail man, became ill and suffered greatly from that time until his death on October 23, 1881.

In 1875, Walter Grieve, John McGregor and others, as directors of the General Protestant Academy, transferred the deed of assignment to the Rev. Thomas Hall. The academy was now under the directorship of Rev. Hall and remained so until 1880 when the reverend gentleman transferred the school over to Emily and Matilda Good in trust for educational purposes in connection with the Congregational Church. The General Protestant Academy then became the St. John's Training School under the direction of the two sisters who were both dedicated church workers. They instructed teachers for the Congregational parish schools throughout Newfoundland for more than 25 years.

The directors of the Training School were Lionel T. Chancey and Robert Barnes as of September 13, 1886. There was one more change made in the directorate on May 2, 1892, when William Martin and Thomas J. Duley were elected to the positions of directors.

In 1904, Miss Helen Jane Laird took over the property and as of that date both the Presbyterian and Congregational interests in the school came to a close. Miss Laird died in late 1918 and in probate of her will, the estate passed to Margaret Snow.

On February 15, 1919, Margaret Snow sold the property to Sir Michael Cashin who had the old buildings demolished in preparation for the construction of his newly planned residence. However, he purchased the Ryan house on Circular Road and having no further use for the Monkstown Road property, he sold it to Mrs. Maud Leamon on May 20, 1920.

Mrs. Leamon had a beautiful home built on the land with landscaped gardens. It was her residence up to the time of her death in 1947. In probate of her will, the property passed to Hilda Crane as of July 17, 1947. When Mrs. Crane died in 1961, the property was purchased by James Greene, Q.C. who is the present owner.

A book titled *The Dissenting Church of Christ at St. John's*, a near-complete history of the Congregational Church of Newfoundland, is highly recommended reading for anyone interested in Newfoundland church history studies.

X

The Private Schools of Georgestown

There appeared in the *St. John's Morning Chronicle* of July 21, 1877 issue, the following advertisement:

> The Misses Murray beg to intimate that, by arrangement with Miss Scott, they have arranged to continue the Ladies School so efficiently conducted by her at Gower Street.

The School will re-open after the mid-summer holidays, on August 1st, 1877, and it is hoped that the new proprietors will be favoured with a share of public confidence and support.

At the outset this public notice had no bearing on matters concerning Georgestown. However, a series of events that happened over the next three years had far-reaching educational effects in the old community.

Amelia, Clara and Jessie Murray, daughters of the late James (1810-64) and Elizabeth (1817-1904) Murray, were sent to Edinburgh in about 1869 to finish their education. Amelia went on to Wiesbaden, Germany in the year 1871, to further her studies while her sisters finished their courses in Scotland. They returned to St. John's in the early summer of 1875 and resided at the family estate "Bellevue" off Rennie's Mill Road. It was expected that the sisters would enter the teaching profession, either on the staff of the Church of England Diocesan Girls School, or with the Presbyterian Academy. They chose, instead, to take over the private school of Miss Scott, who, due to failing health, decided to close out her school on Gower Street.

At that time, Miss Scott's pupils numbered 91 girls enrolled at her institution of learning.

The Murray sisters, with the aid of their brother James, planned on erecting a new schoolhouse on Fleming Street. This building, it was said, was to be named "Birchwood House" as a monument to their sister Anna who died in Scotland while attending school in the town of Moffat in the year 1871.

Although the land was purchased and the building completed by 1879 it was never opened as the Murray Sisters School for Young Ladies. The name selected for the schoolhouse was never to appear on the building, because by that date two of the founding sisters had married and the sole remaining teacher of the trio had planned her wedding day for the year 1880.

Amelia married John Anderson (the father of Daylight Saving Time in Newfoundland) in the year 1877. Her sister Jessie became the wife of Nels Ohman, a Swede. The Ohmans moved to Montreal to live. Clara married George Archibald, a Nova Scotian who was employed with a St. John's mercantile firm. They moved to Pictou County in Nova Scotia within the year.

It was said that the Murray girls conducted the best young ladies school in St. John's for the three years their institution was in operation, and the young students were all looking forward to the opening of the new school facilities which was to take place in the new school year, in August of 1881. With the decision to close out the Murray School and to sell the new building on Fleming Street, prospects for the leading young ladies school looked gloomy.

However, a Mrs. E. Barnes decided to approach Miss Clara Murray with the purpose of taking over the Gower Street School. Apparently an agreement was reached, for in the October 5, 1880 issue of the *Evening Telegram* the following advertisement was printed:

Mrs. E. Barnes, assisted by her daughters, intends continuing the Ladies School at present conducted by Miss Murray, and is prepared to give instructions in the usual branches of a sound English education. Music, Drawing and Perspective Landscape and Flower Painting, and French will be taught as extras. School will open on 4 Nov. 1880 under our direction.

Mrs. Barnes, widow of Ebenezer Barnes (1821-1873), now became the proprietor of the Ladies School on Gower Street. She was capably assisted in this venture by her daughters, Hannah and Sophia. They conducted classes in the most efficient manner. This resulted in an increase in enrolment which brought the total to more than 100 pupils within a span of two years. At this point the teaching staff had to be increased and a bigger building was necessary to house the school. Mrs. Barnes retired from active teaching duties and her daughter, Hannah, became the new proprietor.

When the 1882 school year ended, Miss Hannah Barnes approached the owner of the Fleming Street building (the one erected in 1879 to house the prospective school for the Murray sisters), now vacant. The owner, Mr. James Murray, consented, after several meetings, to transfer ownership to Miss Barnes and her sister, Sophia. Necessary papers were drawn up and finalized for the school opening in this new schoolhouse on September 3, 1883. Desks, chairs, tables, blackboards and all related school equipment were moved to the Fleming Street building, and more equipment had to be purchased on the shortest notice in order to have the classrooms ready for the opening date. Although the school on Gower Street was for young ladies, the new facilities on Fleming Street provided for the admission of boys, and the school that was to open in September became known as "The Barnes Private School for Youth" (young ladies and gentlemen).

The Barnes Private School gained in popularity and soon thereafter, the enrolment soared to more than 130 students. Most of the new pupils came from Georgestown. To keep their school standards high, the Misses Barnes hired many teachers with top-rate credits. Most came from Great Britain Teacher Training institutions, but many were also graduates from the St. John's

Training School (conducted by the Good sisters) on Monkstown Road.

Miss Hannah Barnes relinquished the proprietorship to her sister, Sophia, in or about the year 1887, when she became the wife of Mr. J.B. Mitchell of St. John's. The new proprietor carried on the running of the school in the same efficient manner as was practiced by her predecessors.

Many of St. John's young lads and lassies obtained a superb education within the walls of the Barnes Private School from 1883 through the years to 1905 when the institution was closed down due to the failing health of the proprietor, Miss Sophia Barnes.

In all probability, the most famous Dancing School in St. John's was that of Mr. John Donnelly and located on Mullock Street, in Georgestown. Mr. Donnelly gave lessons to those who sought his instruction, and no one was refused admission to his dance studio.

Mr. Donnelly opened his dance school in 1889, at which time he built a large extension to his residence which was his ballroom studio. Donnelly was a superb dance master and his lessons were so well given that nearly all of his pupils could dance the difficult quadrilles, lancers and gavottes, polkas and other set dances that were popular at that time. All of Donnelly's dance courses took approximately 50 hours and were given three nights a week, the courses being completed in five weeks.

Mr. Donnelly is credited with being the first to give lessons in the famous dances. "Schottische" was a round or set dance in double measure, similar to a polka but slower in tempo. It was partly of Scottish origin and the beat was in three-quarter time. "Mazurka" was a Polish country dance in moderate triple measure. The music for this group (set) dance was always in a moderate three-eight tempo, but Donnelly gave lessons in this dance, to his more advanced students, in three-quarter time as he considered it a better tempo for this dance. "Sir Roger de Couverly" was a round dance or square dance in which partners "step it out" in turns until the fourth couple have completed their set. The dance then went into a circle or round step. It was usually in either three-eighth or three-quarter, and Mr. Donnelly always saw to it that every class member took part in this dance as part of the course for it was one of the fashionable dances of the high-class balls that were held throughout old St. John's in the late 1800s and early decades of the twentieth century.

He gave lessons in the most popular dance, the waltz, especially those styled to the Vienna Waltzes, set to the music of the waltz king, Strauss, which were the main dances of all the great balls of the era. Mr. Donnelly was usually in the forefront of the Grand March whenever he would attend one of the many balls that were held in the Mechanics Hall. He always said that the ballroom of that club was the best dance floor in St. John's and he gave the reason that it was a well-kept and highly polished hardwood floor that could accommodate more than 100 couples with enough space on which to carry out all the movements of the set dances and waltzes with ease.

Mr. Donnelly was also one of St. John's finer cricketers. In his time, he played with the Shamrock Cricket Club and when they won the championship, he displayed the trophy in the dance studio of his residence on Mullock Street as there were no set clubrooms for its display. It was approved by all the players on the team because they all took lessons at his dance school.

There was a small private school on Hayward Avenue in the early decades of the twentieth century that was more or less a children's school. The proprietor was Mrs. Walkins, who was ably assisted in the teaching of the pupils by her daughters, Misses Bride, Bridget and Anastasia. The fee was 40 cents per week and classes were held from 9:00 A.M. to 11:00 A.M. for those as first year students. All other classes, up to what would nowadays be Grade Two were held from 9:00 A.M. to noon and 2:00 to 3:00 P.M. Children were taught to read, write, and recite poems, and draw geometric figures, and the school always had a prize day. The big event of the school year closed out with a series of plays given by the pupils of all classes—Kindergarten to Grade (Book) Two.

From this little private school the students would graduate to, at least, Grade Two in the major denominational schools of the city. The school closed in or about the year 1921.

Mrs. Cleary operated a young ladies and gents dancing school at about the same time as that of the Mrs. Walkins Children's School. Mrs. Cleary's school was on Monkstown Road. There she gave lessons in basic ballet and children's dancing form. Her senior pupils were instructed in light ballet while the intermediate classes were taught the various steps of the Minuet. Lessons were given in the Sir Roger de Couverly and other set or folk dances that could be performed by younger folk.

One of her preferences in dance instruction was that of the English country dances. She excelled in the teaching of these as well as the gavottes and waltzes that her young charges would perform. Her graduation classes would stage a performance on prize day, which was always a social event of note.

Mrs. Cleary's Dance School closed in or about the year 1931.

A small nursery (preschool age) school was opened up in the 1904 to 1913 years by a Mrs. Smith-Martin. The school was located in her Belvedere Street residence and catered to the preschool children of four to five years of age. Her husband was transferred to Michigan by his company and Mrs. Smith-Martin closed out her nursery school in May 1913.

XI

Belvedere

An early map of St. John's, dated 1751, shows a large plantation on the "Barrens" north of the town. This property is believed to be the plantation granted to a William John McKie, a senior officer of His Majesty's Forces stationed in St. John's and halfway through his final term (six years) of duty in the military service of Great Britain. His son, Peter, inherited the estate upon the death of his father, believed to be in or about 1773. Peter was then 23 years of age and employed as the Surveyor of Customs for the Port (St. John's).

The place then known as "McKie's Grove," which was later to become "Belvedere," was quite an extensive property. It was bounded on the south by Arundel Cottage Road (now known as Newtown Road) and on the north by the road to Upper Long Pond, later known as Allandale Road. (Today the thoroughfare is called Bonaventure Avenue.) McKie's estate encompassed about 20 acres of land, a large land holding in old St. John's. Most of the plantation was composed of highly productive agricultural rolling meadowland and vegetable-producing fields. The site of the McKie Cottage or mansion was in a small grove of trees that formed a secluded shelter from the harsh easterly winds of spring. The small grove also acted as a shield against the cold northerly and westerly winds and gales in wintertime.

The house was a large two-storey structure with a steep gabled roof. The roof line was broken by three gabled dormer-type windows facing westward. Two windows of the same style broke the steep slant of the east side of the roof. Like all the other plantation houses in St. John's, the servants of the mansion had their quarters in the attic section of the building.

In the year 1821, Peter McKie sold his St. John's estate to Hugh Emerson. McKie had retired from his position as Surveyor of Customs in St. John's for which he was to receive a yearly pension. However, he now accepted the appointment as Magistrate for Bay Bulls and moved there to carry out his new duties in that place. Peter McKie resided in Bay Bulls for the next 15 years before he died on April 5, 1836. He is buried in the Church of England cemetery there. The following notice of his passing appeared in the *St. John's Times*:

> Died: on Wednesday last, aged 88 years, Peter McKie Esq., native of North Britain, who for upwards of fifty years held the situation of Surveyor of His Majesty's Customs at the port (St. John's) and who for the last fifteen years has been on the superannuation list.

Hugh Emerson, having purchased the McKie estate, resided in the old McKie house for approximately five years. In 1826 Hugh hired the services of Alexander Norris to design and build a new house which was to be erected almost 600 feet east of the McKie house. This new location would make the new residence closer to the more travelled road to Upper Long Pond. The path over which the building materials were transported later became the private driveway to Emerson's Belvedere Mansion.

The new house was nearing completion when fire broke out in the old McKie house. The fire was believed to have started in the kitchen and spread rapidly through the north section of the structure. Since the hired hands (farm workers in the nearby field) quickly fought the blaze, only a section of the second floor and a roof at the north end of the house suffered major damage. As it was early summer Emerson had necessary repairs carried out to make the place suitable for habitation until he could move into the new house, which was to be completed in early August of that year.

On August 15, 1827, the Emerson family moved into their new mansion. The grounds surrounding the residence had been grassed into lawns, flower beds were in bloom and the many and varied shrubs were in flower. The driveway had been fenced and the trees imported from Nova Scotia, England and the U.S., having been planted in early spring, were now completely cloaked in leaf. Under ideal weather the Emersons celebrated the occasion of the opening of their Belvedere mansion with a private garden party that started at 11:00 A.M. and continued through the afternoon. At night the invited friends and guests took part in a ball held within the spacious halls and rooms of "Belvedere." All were attired in the appropriate evening apparel used in such social events of that era.

The new building was styled in the fashion of the typical plantation-manor houses of western Nova Scotia. Hugh Emerson titled his estate "Belvedere," the same name his father gave his plantation in Windsor, N.S. when the Empire Loyalist moved there from Concord, Massachusetts U.S.A. in the year 1744. Although "Belvedere" was now the official name of Hugh Emerson's estate many of the citizens of old St. John's continued to call it by the original "McKie's Grove" title. It was only after the estate was purchased by Bishop Fleming that the name

"Belvedere" became a household name throughout St. John's, because in the year 1848 the good bishop opened part of the western fields as the new Catholic burial ground and named it "Belvedere Cemetery."

The old McKie house became the residence of the chief farmer whose duties consisted of keeping the lawns and flowering beds well cared for, as well as seeing to the cultivation of the fields. Crop harvesting and the care of livestock was a year-round work that required a full-time staff of more than three employees. "Belvedere" became one of the best farms in St. John's because of the calibre of the employees that Mr. Emerson hired to run his plantation.

After the death of his wife in the year 1844, Hugh Emerson retired from the practice of law and from public life. He sold his "Belvedere" to the Rt. Rev. Michael Anthony Fleming, Bishop of St. John's in the year 1847. The next year he left St. John's with his daughter and went to London, England to live.

The following notice appeared in both the *Public Ledger* and the *Times* newspapers of St. John's in their July 13, 1860 issues:

> Died: In London, England, on May 29, 1860, Hugh Emerson Esq., late Solicitor General of the Colony.

Bishop Fleming made Emerson's "Belvedere" his official residence as of November 1, 1847 and moved into occupancy at the end of the month. His Lordship carried on all church business from his new residence. As he knew of the planned legislation to close all graveyards inside St. John's, the good bishop set plans in motion for an early start in converting a section of the western fields of his estate into a new Catholic burial grounds. On July 4,

1848, the Bishop officially named it "Belvedere Cemetery." Although many bodies were exhumed at the old Catholic burial grounds off Long's Hill and reinterred in the new cemetery, it is believed that a young girl, Kattie Eagan by name, and who died of an unknown disease, was the first corpse to be buried in "Belvedere Cemetery." The burial is said to have taken place sometime in early August of that year.

A John Carroll, from the neighbourhood of Waterford County, Ireland, who celebrated his one hundred and fifth birthday in January of 1848, died in July of that year and was buried in Belvedere Cemetery. His grave marker is near the entry gate at the end of the "Belvedere Driveway," and is greatly deteriorated by the weather and badly damaged by vandals in recent years. It is evidence that his could have actually been the first corpse to be interred in Belvedere Cemetery.

In the following year Bishop Fleming introduced to St. John's a Third Order of Franciscan Brothers to teach at the Orphans' Asylum operated by the B.I.S. The Brothers, although they wore the brown habit of the Franciscan Monks, were not bound by religious vows. The Bishop built a monastery for them at Belvedere and they resided there. The experiment did not work out, and by midsummer of 1853 the Monastery closed down with the last of the Brothers returning to Galway, Ireland. In 1842 the Bishop had introduced the Sisters of Mercy to St. John's. At that time their duties were to visit the sick and poor and to help alleviate their sufferings. They also were to teach a higher level of education to the young Catholic girls of St. John's, but all religious denominations were welcome to have their young girls enter the school to gain the benefits of the improved methods of higher education being imparted by the Sisters.

Bishop Fleming was, at this time, in failing health so he requested an assistant to help him with the work of running the

Catholic Church in Newfoundland. Fr. John Thomas Mullock O.S.F. was selected, and appointed co-adjutant. On December 27, 1847, he was elevated to a Bishop. He arrived in St. John's on May 6, 1848, and took up his duties as assistant to Bishop Fleming without further delay. Although it was Bishop Fleming's plan, the new Bishop saw to the building of two convents, a new Palace, an Episcopal Library and the completion of the Catholic Cathedral. Bishop Fleming died July 14, 1850, and Bishop Mullock became his successor as head of the Catholic Church in Newfoundland.

Bishop Mullock's first task was the building of the first Catholic girls orphanage. It was to the north side of Mercy Convent on Military Road and opened December 8, 1854. His next project was the founding of St. Bonaventure's College. The college was first housed in the old Palace on Henry Street while the new building was being erected on lately acquired property known as Halley's Cottage Grounds. This property was adjacent to the Williams Plantation that the late Bishop Fleming had obtained in the year 1838. The first President of St. Bonaventure's College was the Rt. Rev. Henry Carfagnini.

On November 16, 1859, the orphanage on Military Road was closed out and the 30 orphans were transferred to "Belvedere," the home of the late Bishop Fleming. The late Bishop left his property and home including the Third Order of Franciscan Monks Monastery to the Sisters of Mercy for the maintenance of the Orphanage. A two-storey building was added November 16, 1859.

Bishop Mullock died March 29, 1869, and was succeeded by the Rt. Rev. John Thomas Power.

Bishop Power's first act was to enlarge "Belvedere Cemetery." He purchased the property of Michael Allen. The acreage was situated on the south side of the proposed Reid Newfoundland Railway and was adjacent to the "Belvedere

Cemetery." The new ground was consecrated July 4, 1881. In the year 1884, the new St. Michael's Orphanage, a fireproof building at Belvedere, was opened. The old wooden building was converted to a barn to house the cattle and other animals that supplied the needs of the orphanage operation. The second floor was used for the storage of hay and animal feeds to sustain the cattle during winter months. The old McKie house was also torn down during the episcopate of Bishop Power.

It was Bishop Power who brought the Irish Christian Brothers to St. John's as teachers of the B.I.S. Schools. Other buildings erected during this tenure of office were the Christian Brothers Monastery at "Mount St. Francis" on Bonaventure Avenue and the Chapel of the Sacred Heart at Mercy Convent on Military Road.

Bishop Power died December 4, 1893 and was succeeded by Michael Francis Howley who was consecrated Bishop on June 24, 1892.

Bishop Howley took office the year following the Great Fire of St. John's. The new Bishop was the first native-born priest to be elevated to Catholic Bishop in Newfoundland. Most of his episcopate was taken up with major repairs, externally, to the Cathedral (now the Basilica of St. John the Baptist) and the rebuilding of Catholic schools burnt in the Fire of 1892. He erected a Mortuary Chapel in Belvedere Cemetery in the year 1901. (This Chapel was burnt to the ground in mid-July 1934. No new chapel has been built to replace it, and is not likely to be, since the cemetery has been closed for future burials except for families who have plots with unused burial space.) He was elevated to Archbishop in 1904. In the year 1907, Archbishop Howley turned the first sod for the extension of St. Bonaventure's College, which was now under the administration of the Irish Christian Brothers. The Archbishop died in the year 1914 and was succeeded by Archbishop Edward Patrick Roche.

Soon after the Irish Christian Brothers arrived in Newfoundland, Bishop Thomas Power planned a residence on Merrymeeting Road. The monastery was designed after the Christian Brothers' Monastery in Wexford, Ireland. The cornerstone of Mount St. Francis Monastery, was laid in September 1877. (Courtesy of the Archives of the R.C. Archdiocese c. 1890)

The old mansion of Hugh Emerson is today St. Michael's Mercy Convent, Belvedere. His highly productive agricultural fields of yesteryear are now covered by a girls' Regional High School (Holy Heart of Mary), a girls' dormitory (McAuley Hall), a convent (St. Catherine's Presentation Convent) and the parking lots for their use just about utilize the entire south or upper section of his estate. Brother Rice High School (boys) and the new Monastery (Brother Rice) take up nearly all the lower fields of the plantation. The field that used to be the site of the Annual Belvedere Garden Party is slowly being transformed into Botanical Gardens through the efforts of the Brothers of Brother Rice Monastery in conjunction with the St. John's Roman Catholic School Board as their administration and maintenance headquarters. A small school for girls and the Catholic Action Centre also occupy parts of the old building.

The following poem by a Mr. W.J. Carey tells of the beauty and tranquility of Belvedere:

BELVEDERE

*My fleeting fancy call to
mind
Were in school-boy days I'd
haunt,
Of things and places left
behind,
Fond memories doth
enchant.
As I think on my youthful
home,
It's fields and foliage rare,
Before I strayed o'er ocean*

foam
From vernal Belvedere.

And o'ft fond musings show
the place,
Now crumbled to decay,
Where the school-boys of
Master Grace
Hath whiled the time away.
In hunting for the feathered
tribe,
Or plucking flowers fair,
As Flora's mantle decked
the field
Of vernal Belvedere.

I've wandered in the Isle of
Saints,
My father's native home,
From Rock of Cashill, old
and quaint,
To where Avoca foam
I've gazed upon fair
mountain scenes
and Etna's burning glare.
In fancy in my midnight
dreams
I visit Belvedere.

I was bronzed beneath the
Africa sun,
Saw many a funeral car,

Where shot and shell and
many fell,
In thunder bursts of war.
But yet; at night, in dreams
delight,
And Etna's burning clear,
Where birds did sing in
blooming spring,
Near vernal Belvedere.

Yon mocking winds that
wafted me
Far from this peaceful
scene,
Adrift on life's delusive sea,
To stem fates changing
theme,
Swift on light arrows bring
to me
Notes from the warblers
there,
That chant with voices
sweetly
Near vernal Belvedere.

I've sported near the
water falls,
That flung their silvery
sprays,
And viewed the church and
gorgeous halls
Of Pompiis, pagan days.

In the Georgestown neighbourhood, many families maintained a small vegetable garden. At the rear of the Presentation Convent on Military Road, the Sisters of the Presentation Congregation maintained an extensive vegetable garden. Archbishop Roche poses with some of the Presentation Sisters in their garden. (Courtesy of the Archives of the Roman Catholic Archdiocese c. 1945)

Have seen where many a
Christian died
By the gladiators spear,
But all their beauty is out-
vied,
In vernal Belvedere.

Yon peril of ethereal space,
Absorbed in heaven's
decree,
That wander through
celestial grace
In pellucid infinity.
Draw back your frown, sin
drawath down,
And shed your rays clear,
With radiance bloom and
myrrh perfume,
On vernal Belvedere.
May zephyrs from sweet
nature's God,
Such as Arch Angels wear;
Enchant the souls beneath
the sod
That sleep in Belvedere.
May virgins grace bedew
each face
Washed in celestial
streams,
Entrance them in eternity,
In Heavenly Golden
Dreams.

Belvedere Convent, or St. Michael's Convent, was constructed in 1827. The building was originally a private home but was purchased by the Church in the 1840s. It served as a residence and orphanage until the 1880s. At that point, the second of the two Belvedere properties was constructed, the brick Belvedere Orphanage. The Orphanage is a three-storey brick structure constructed in 1884-1885. Belvedere Convent is the third-oldest building in St. John's. It is historically linked to the Emerson family, and was the deathplace of Bishop Fleming. (Courtsey of the Archives of the R.C. Archdiocese of St. John's c.1900)

Mr. Carey remembered when Belvedere Cemetery was known as McKie's Grove. The last time he saw it was in the summer of 1858.

XII

St. Bonaventure's: Newfoundland's First College

The first five years of Bishop Mullock's episcopate were devoted to the completion of the monumental workload instituted by his predecessor (Bishop Fleming who died July 14, 1850). Having completed and consecrated the Cathedral of St. John the Baptist (now the Basilica of St. John the Baptist), His Lordship began work on his own plans for the well-being of his flock in matters of Catholic education and social services for all.

In early August of the year 1855, the Bishop purchased at public auction a huge supply of cut granite stone blocks. They had been brought out from Waterford, Ireland for the building of a new penitentiary. The penal institution was planned by the Legislative Assembly, but before it was completed, Responsible Government was granted Newfoundland. The new form of government was now running the affairs of state and they decided to cut back on the size of the new gaol in order to better use the money on more-needy services at public expenditure. The excess granite blocks were therefore sold at public auction. There were more than 30,000 of the specially cut building stones in the lot.

In the meantime, His Lordship had begun negotiations for the purchase of the Halley Cottage and grounds which were adjacent to the property on which the new Palace and Cathedral were built (that property was formerly known as the Williams Plantation which was obtained by the late Bishop Fleming in the year 1838). The Halley Cottage and grounds were finally obtained and the deeds pertaining to that land grant were legally settled by mid-October. With the purchases of the granite building stones and the Halley Cottage and grounds, the Bishop announced his plans for an institute of higher learning. The recent acquisitions were to be used for the main building and site for its campus.

On December 1, 1856, the college was officially founded and formally opened by Bishop Mullock. It was the first college in Newfoundland and His Lordship named it St. Bonaventure's College in honour of the Franciscan Order's most scholarly and outstanding Saint next only to that Order's founder, and because the late Bishop (Fleming) died July 14, 1850, the feast day of St. Bonaventure. As the plans for the new building were still in the drawing stages, the first classes for the enrolled students were conducted in the old Palace located on Henry Street, under the direction of the College President, Rev. Fr. Carfagini, an Italian priest who was later to become the Bishop of Harbour Grace. The college operated out of the old Palace until the new building was completed on the chosen site in the year 1858.

In April of 1857, Bishop Mullock laid the cornerstone for the first St. Bonaventure's building on the new campus (formerly Halley's Cottage and Grounds). The college was instituted as a seminary for the development of vocations to the priesthood and religious life. Courses were carried out in strict adherence to the standards of universities on the European continent. When the Bishop founded the college, he opened an era of educational enlightenment that brought Newfoundland into the realms of

Arts and Letters courses comparable with those granted by universities throughout the world.

The new building was completed in March 1858 and the transition from the old Palace took only a few days with little interruption of classes and studies. Dormitories were installed in the new building over the summer, and boarder students were accommodated when the college reopened for classes in September. The institution was basically a seminary where non-clerical students were admitted in the early years which led to the decision by the Bishop to change the regulations in 1868 whereby the college accepted all prospective students who could pass the entry examinations. When classes opened in the autumn, the successful candidates became "Bonaventurans." Many of them were non-Catholic.

Bishop Mullock, the founder of St. Bonaventure's College, died March 29, 1869. Dr. Power, his successor, became the new Bishop. He appointed Fr. Lovejoy for President with a free hand to run the college. The teaching staff was completed with the additions of Fr. Lynch, Mr. Talbot, Mr. Fitzpatrick, Mr. O'Regan and Professor Bennett, who was the music teacher. (Professor McLaurin and Mr. Fanclon were on the staff since 1858. They had served with every president up to this date.) However, ten years later in 1879, Bishop Power requested the Irish Christian Brothers to take over the teaching duties and administration of the college.

The institution was founded by a Franciscan (Bishop Mullock) and run by priests of that Order for the first 14 years and produced more than 30 native-born priests and almost that amount who entered religious life either as monks or brothers. Many of the non-cleric graduates became active in the affairs of state, or in the professional and commercial life of the country. The high standards of excellence that the Franciscan Fathers

Sixteen years after the cornerstone was laid for the Cathedral of St. John the Baptist, Bishop John Thomas Mullock held the consecration mass on September 9, 1855. In recognition of its exceptional artistic, architectural and historical importance, Pope Pius XII designated the Cathedral a minor basilica, the word "Basilica" meaning "Royal Hall." (Courtesy of Maura Hanrahan)

molded at St. Bonaventure's were now passed over to the Irish Christian Brother to uphold.

The first President under this new administration was Rev. Bro. J.L. Slattery. He was ably assisted by Bros. Pendergast and Crehan who came to St. Bonaventure's with him. Bro. Culhane joined the staff in the following year. Shortly thereafter, Mr. Conroy, later to become a Judge of the Supreme Court of Newfoundland, was added to the teaching staff. The winter months' activities, class debating, public lectures on scientific and cultural matters, the dramatic portraits, by students, of the plays of Shakespeare so that all could better understand the works of the great writer, were continued under this new administration.

The fame of the college, academically, in athletics and drama grew in leaps and bounds. Its enrolment took on an international look as students of many foreign lands took up studies within the now famous institution. Just before the Great Fire of 1892, Professor Hutton joined the staff at St. Bonaventure's. He produced many plays, operas, operettas such as "Ali Baba," "The Merchant of Venice," and the operetta "Pied Piper" to name but a few, using only students as the actors. He conducted the orchestras as well as the direction and general supervision all dramatic productions at the college well into the late 1920s. In the year 1901, Sidney Herbert was the first winner of the Rhodes Scholarship for Newfoundland. A.M. Power won the Jubilee Scholarship for the year 1902; in the following year G.S. White took the award. It marked the first time that a college won two consecutive Jubilee Scholarships. Of the first nine such scholarships, St. Bonaventure's won four of them.

Sometime in the spring of the year 1916, the classroom occupied by the Junior Matriculation students became non-functional. The electric circuitry and heating system failed in that section of the building. Maintenance crews were summoned but were unable to remedy the malfunctions by noon hour. The President immediately moved the boys to another class so that classes would go on without further delay because the students would be writing the London Matriculation examination papers in late June.

There was a small room on the main floor of the college that was used for religious instructions for young boys preparing to receive their first Holy Communion. This room was located to the right and in the shadow of the main stairway in the new wing that had been added to the college in the year 1907. The Junior Matriculation class was composed of 12 students, so this room was most adequate as a substitute until their classroom would be ready for use.

One morning a boarding student and member of the class, Philip Lewis by name, went into the substitute classroom, at about 8:00 A.M., and drew a picture of a fully-rigged four-masted ship. The drawing was done on a pale pink painted wall. Lewis's masterpiece was done with coloured chalks and stood out so vividly that when the teacher (the College President) saw the drawing, he forbade anyone to erase the Lewis work of art. Philip Lewis named his creation *Ocean Queen,* and from that day the little room was known as *The Ocean Queen.* In about the year 1937, the room was converted to a book supply centre by the college. However, by that date the Lewis masterpiece had long faded away.

The President, Bro. J.F. Ryan called a general assembly in the Aula Maxima on the morning of May 7, 1922 to announce that plans were drawn up to construct an indoor skating and hockey rink for winter sporting activities at the college. The cost was outlined in brief and plans were soon underway to raise funds to defray the construction costs. The Alumni Association, the Ladies Auxiliary and the students all pitched in to raise money in various ways. The rink was built by a lot of free labour and completed in time for opening in 1923. It was a gala affair to say the least. All the students skated onto the ice dressed in costumes of Cavaliers, Pirates, Santa Clauses, Pioneers, Sailors, Sinbad, Ali Baba, Little Jack Horner, Boy Blue, Miners, Fishermen, Loggers, Firemen, Policemen and Chimney Sweeps.

The rink had an oval for skating and inside the oval, properly fenced off, an area for hockey games. The oval was later taken out and the ice surface lengthened for a longer playing area. (When the Arena burnt down in 1940 the St. Bonaventure's College rink substituted as the Senior League competition area until better accommodations were built in 1953.) In the year 1928, a college team composed of Billy Cotter, Herman Quigley, Ed Kennedy, Allan Johnston, Gerry Hanley, Ed English, Barney Kennedy, George Dwyer and Brian White played the Halifax Crescents to a three to three draw in a game played in the college rink.

St. Bonaventure's College has had a glorious record in intercollegiate athletic competitions down through the years, but the most outstanding victory ever recorded was that of the Dominion Sports Meet of 1920. The competition was between the three city colleges. Under the auspicies of the C.C.C. Boat Club, the meet was held in the then Prince's Rink on November 23, 1920. The indoor Track and Field events of competition were quarter-mile, half-mile, and mile races, high jump, senior and junior relay races. Each college was permitted to enter three competitors in each event. Three points and a gold medal were awarded to the winner, second place was awarded two points and a silver medal and the third place finisher got one point. The college accumulating the most points was to be presented

The field in front of St. Bonaventure's College was frozen every winter to allow for winter recreation for the students of the College. Neighbourhood children from the Georgestown area often came to watch and play a few games of hockey. Directly behind the students is the Basilica Museum and Library, The Bishops palace and the Basilica Cathedral. (Courtsey of the Archives of the Roman Catholic Archdiocese c. 1904)

with a cup that was for permanent possession. The college team of E. Phalen, E. Maher, F. O'Brien, W. Skinner, R. Halley, G. Murphy, G. Eagan, A. Collins, M. Stoyles, J. Howlett, C. Eagan, G. Lynch and A. Slattery won the meet. They won first, second and third places in every race and in the high jump, and they took first place in both relays thereby securing the maximum of points.

In the year 1957 under the presidency of Rev. Bro. J.B. Darcy, the third building was erected at the north end of the campus to accommodate the large influx of students to the college. It was the last major project to be undertaken at the great institution. In 1962 the Regional High School System was introduced to St. John's and Newfoundland by the government of the day. St. Bonaventure's was relegated to the status of a grade school. By this act the glorious history of the first college in Newfoundland came to an end as an institute of higher learning serving Newfoundlanders. Over its life span of 106 years, the college as an institute of learning and athletic accomplishments was world-famous. It produced a baron, knight, prime ministers, governors, archbishops, bishops, Chief Justices, missionaries to foreign lands, Justices, ambassadors, military heroes, top-rate surgeons and physicians, and anything one can think to name, a Bonaventurian can be found in that field of endeavour.

Listed below are the names of all the Presidents of St. Bonaventure's College:

1st: Archbishop H. Carfagini, 1856-1863
2nd: Very Rev. M. Walsh, 1863-1866
3rd: Very Rev. T. McGrath, 1866-1869
4th: Very Rev. J. Lovejoy, 1869-1872
5th: Very Rev. P. Slattery, 1872-1877

6th: Very Rev. W. Fitzpatrick, 1877-1883
7th: Very Rev. M. Fitzgerald, 1883-1888
8th: Very Rev. W. Ahern, 1888-1889.

The first eight presidents of St. Bonaventure's College were priests of the Franciscan Order. All, with the exception of Archbishop Carfagini (an Italian), were Irishmen. Only one, Very Rev. T. McGrath, who died June 2, 1877, is buried in Belvedere Cemetery.

9th: Rev. Bro. J.L. Slattery, 1889-1891
10th: Rev. Bro. J.J. Crehan, 1891-1896
11th: Rev. Bro. G.B. Lovelle, 1896-1901
12th: Rev. Bro. J.J. Downey, 1901-1903
13th: Rev. Bro. P.J. Culhane, 1903-1912
14th: Rev. Bro. J.B. Ryan, 1912-1921
15th: Rev. Bro. J.F. Ryan, 1921-1927
16th: Rev. Bro. P.B. Doyle, 1927-1928
17th: Rev. Bro. M.C. Ahern, 1928-1931
18th: Rev. Bro. J.V. Birmingham, 1931-1937
19th: Rev. Bro. W.K.. O'Connell, 1937-1941
20th: Rev. Bro. J.V. Birmingham, 1941-1944
21st: Rev. Bro. A.B. Knight, 1944-1947
22nd: Rev. Bro. P.C. Fleming, 1947-1953
23rd: Rev. Bro. H.P. Tarrant, 1953-1956
24th: Rev. Bro. J.B. Darcy, 1956-1960
25th: Rev. Bro. J.J. Enright, 1960-1962

Rev. Bro. A.B. Knight was the first Newfoundland-born President of the College. Bros. H.P. Tarrant and J.B. Darcy are the only other native-born Presidents of the College.

Rev. Bro. P.B. Doyle held the post of President when the London Matriculation examination papers were written by the Senior Associate Students for the last time at St. Bonaventure's College.

Although St. Bonaventure's is now a grade school, the great spirit built over the years has not diminished in the hearts and minds of the present-day students.

XIII

The New York Circus Comes to St. John's

There appeared in the newspapers of St. John's for Thursday, September 16, 1847, the following announcement:

The New York Circus

Rockwell & Co.—Proprietors

C.R. Banks—Manager

The proprietors of this noted Establishment have the pleasure of announcing to the gentry and inhabitants of St. John's and the outports, that they have made arrangements for giving a series of:

Equestrian and Gymnastic

Entertainments,

in St. John's, to commence about the 22nd Inst. (due notice, however, will be given of the time of first performance.)

The establishment is well and favourably known in the United States, Canada, New

Brunswick, Nova Scotia, and the West Indies, where it has received extensive patronage and the manager trusts it will be conducted in such a manner as to win the approval of the inhabitants of Newfoundland.

Attached to the concern are an efficient corps of Equestrian and Gymnastic Performers, Pantominists, Negro Medallists, a fine stud of blood Horses, Trained Ponies, and a Band of Superior Musicians.

The following artists are a portion of the company:

Mrs. D. Johnson, and Miss J.M. Johnson, female Equestrians.

Mr. W.C. Johnson, Mr. J.L. Lipman, Master J. Johnson, and Master Jackman, principal male Equestrians, supported by a corps of Entre Riders, Mr. D. Gardner, and Mr. Callahan, Clowns:—Mr. Leupine, Mr. Smith, and others, Acrobatic Artistes, together with a host of minor performers.

The exhibitions will be given under a spacious travelling pavilion capable of containing 3,000 persons, which will be erected in a field of Mr. Brown's, opposite the residence of Mr. James Bayley, Esq., Monkstown Road.

Admission:

Dress Circle—5 shillings

Boxes—2 shillings, 6 pence

Pit—1 shilling, 3 pence

Doors open at 7:00 P.M. Performance to commence at half past 7 P.M.

Afternoon performances each day, commencing at 3 o'clock.

G.H. Campbell

16 September Advertising Agent

This New York entertainment establishment was the first-ever circus to visit St. John's when they staged their performance September 22, 1847, in their travelling pavilion, which they erected on Robert Brown's field, before a near-capacity audience of more than 2,300 people.

This site, Brown's Field in Georgestown, was an ideal location for the land was almost level, and it was protected from the prevailing winds, with a natural high rising gradual slope to the northwest at the immediate rear of the property. The field was just North of Military Road and fronted on the then Georgestown Road which was a busy thoroughfare that led to the farms and plantations in the Upper Long Pond region, and also to the Queen Victoria Hills fortifications. The Brown's Field of yesteryear is now the site of houses 5, 7, 9, and 11 Monkstown Road, just north of W.J. Murphy Ltd. at the corner of Military and Monkstown Roads, more commonly known as Rawlins Cross.

The land area of Brown's Field was a little more than 14,000 square feet. The travelling pavilion, which was a very big canvas tent (later these types of pavilions were called "The Big Tops" in circus language) took up most of the area. There were caravans in which the performers lived, and other shelters, also on wheels, in which the horses, ponies, and trained dogs were housed. One large caravan was the dining hall for the circus people, who lived like one big family. The main office of the circus was held in this caravan, but the manager had his own private quarters in a smaller caravan.

The roof of the big tent was supported by four main masts (pine poles) 35 feet high. These poles were gauged by four-inch-diameter ropes or hawsers. The roustabouts worked for two days anchoring and erecting the main tent and installing the seating arrangements. The centre section, known as the "main ring," was the area where all the performances were staged, and the entrance ramp to this "ring" was from the west end of the long pavilion. No seat in the tent was set where the view of the performance was obstructed by a pole or roof support. An arrangement of gas lights illuminated the stage or "main ring" and there was ample lighting of the same kind throughout the pavilion. An excellent policing system was maintained throughout the entire stay of this circus company that ensured an orderly conduct of all performances and the protection of the equipment located in Brown's Field.

The first night opening started on time. At 7:30 P.M., all the performers paraded onto the "main ring" to the music of the marching bands, followed by the corps of riders, the featured equestrians, then the ponies with their mounts and trainers. The gymnasts, doing handstands and somersaults, backflips and cartwheels, were followed by the colourfully costumed negro minstrel singers. The ringmaster and circus manager were followed by the pantominists, and handlers and the trained dogs brought up the rear. The band had moved to the section reserved for them while all the performers formed a circle around the ringmaster and the manager. After his opening remarks, the manager thanked the patrons who came to see the night's entertainment. He introduced the ringmaster, who immediately introduced the equestrian act, and the show was on. It was an outstanding performance and ushered in a new form of entertainment to old St. John's that was thereafter well received in the city.

The circus drew large crowds for the first two weeks. By that time most of the acts were seen by the patrons many times over, and the novelty was wearing thin. The crowds dropped to less than 1,000 spectators so the management decided to bring in new shows.

The need for more time to rehearse the acts was too short, so it was announced that as of October 9, 1847, there would only be two afternoon performances a week. They were to be presented on Wednesday and Saturday afternoons and would commence at three o'clock. The new acts would need all the other afternoons to perfect the presentations. The equestrian performances needed to be precise and the aerial acrobatic acts required extra time so that the trapezists could execute their somersaults to the rhythm of the band. Gymnasts had also new acts to perfect.

One of the equestrians, Mr. J.L. Lipman fell while practicing a breathtaking jump. The company had a Farewell Benefit Night for him in which they introduced most of the new acts. The performance was so good and so well received that no acts lasted more than a week. The management found that by making new shows every five days the Circus would draw between 1,800 and 2,300 patrons per show.

As the weather was getting cold and wet at that time of year, the New York Circus staged their last performance in Georgestown to their St. John's patrons on the night of November 12, 1847, before a full house. The manager stood in the "main ring" after the last act and thanked the residents of St. John's for their support for his circus, and promised that should they again visit St. John's, their entertainment would include many more attractions. He concluded his speech by thanking the people for their most friendly attitude to him and all members of the travelling circus.

The crew and performers dismantled their pavilion and lesser tents the next day and by Monday, November 14, 1847, all equipment, animals and caravans were being loaded aboard an outgoing vessel for passage to Kingston, Jamaica, where they were scheduled to perform by November 28, 1847.

It is believed that the New York Circus, which was quite reputable, was purchased by P.T. Barnum in or about the year 1860. However, other sources say that Mr. Bailey purchased the growing concern from the Rockwell & Co. proprietors in the summer of 1856. Bailey ran this circus successfully as he did with the many others that he had purchased over the years. It was said that by the buying of the New York Circus, Bailey was able to bring about his joint venture with the famous P.T. Barnum that became the Barnum and Bailey Circus "The Greatest Show on Earth."

Shortly after the New York Circus left Monkstown Road people began to lease land in that area, and the following spring many new homes were being built on the roadway. This is, today, Catherine Street. James Street (now Mullock Street) was another area that saw new home construction at around this date.

XIV

The Grand Old Man of Georgestown

Mr. Henry Martin, who resides at 28 Williams Street in the Georgestown Section of St. John's, is the city's oldest citizen. Harry, the name by which he has always been known, is 102 years of age as of August 1, 1981. He is the eldest child of the late James and Johanna (Brown) Martin. Both of his parents were born in old St. John's, however, Harry's place of birth was at Little Heart's Ease, Southwest Arm, Trinity Bay.

Harry's father was a boatbuilder by trade, and plied his skills wherever he obtained an order for boat construction. James Martin and his wife moved to Little Heart's Ease in April of the year 1879. Mr. Martin had been hired, by a wealthy fish merchant of that settlement, to build a "Jack" (a small schooner-type vessel) and two "Bait Skiffs." All boats were to be ready for use no later than mid-September of that year. The owner wanted them working the waters of Trinity Bay. From all accounts the merchant wanted to use them on the Labrador in the Spring.

On the first day of August 1879, Harry Martin first saw the light of day in that little settlement. The Martins lived in Little Heart's Ease for the next eight months. They moved across the Arm to a little harbour known as Hatchet Cove, where James Martin built a cottage, wharf and his little boat yard. Martin chose this place because it had an abundance of fine timber that grew right down to the waters of the Arm, and the little cove was sheltered from the bad winds. Although Martin was a boatbuilder by trade, he was also a logger, a farmer, a carpenter and a fisherman. He, like all of the early Newfoundlanders, possessed an inborn industrious trait and a strong determination to succeed in his pioneer life. Two more sons were born to the Martin family before they moved back to St. John's in the year 1884. As it was late in October when they arrived in St. John's, they lived with Mr. Martin's father (in his house) on Signal Hill. In June of the following year their new residence was on Cookstown Road, in a house that Mr. Martin leased from a Miss Carrigan.

While living in this area of St. John's, young Harry met up with young boys who were to become his lifetime companions.

Such lads as Gordy Miller, Willie Miller, Carson Payne and Stevie Brien became his childhood friends, with whom he spent most of his leisure time. The young group became good swimmers, and not a day passed in summer that they did not have a "dip" in Sandy Bottom, a pool carved by nature in a bend on Leary's Brook that flows into the western end of Long Pond. (The old swimming pool was in the area where the Health Sciences Centre on Memorial University Campus now stands.)

On the afternoon of July 8, 1892, the boys were returning from swimming when one of them saw huge billowing clouds of smoke in the sky over the city. As they were walking uphill, they could not see the town until they got to the top of the grade. (Old Newtown Road crossed over the hill and led down to the Sand Pits at the head of Long Pond. That length of road is gone now, but Westerland Road is very near the location of the old road.) Then they saw the holocaust. They ran all the way to the Martin residence only to find it completely gutted by fire. The boys helped Mrs. Martin move the few items of clothing and furniture that she and the younger Martin children salvaged from the flames.

Harry wanted to go downtown to find his father, but his mother prevented him and his companions from doing so. She persuaded them that they were needed at what was left of their homes, for their safety. That night the Martins were all together and found shelter in the basement of a Mrs. Smith's house located on LeMarchant Road. By the week's end, the Martins had shelter in fire-victims accommodations set up on the Parade Grounds, and following that date they were moved to tents erected in Bannerman Park. As nearly all of St. John's East End had been destroyed by the Great Fire, it was almost impossible to purchase or lease housing in the unburnt sections of the city. However, James Martin was successful in leasing a house on the lower section of Springdale Street where his family were reunited under the same roof for the first time in five weeks.

The months following the Great Fire were rough on many, but the Martins were very busy because James, while a boat-builder, now was employed as a carpenter. He was constantly busy in building or repairing homes. He and his brother decided that they would open up their own carpentry business and within a week of their decision, they were building a row of houses in the East End of the city. They also built new houses on Walsh's Square and had moved into them before Christmas. James, being a very thrifty man banked a large share of his earnings for, during the height of the building boom, his son Harry was working with him and an uncle as an assistant carpenter. His earnings also augmented the family budget. The Martins, at last, were a fairly well-to-do family, and the prospects of more building in the new year (1895) gave promise of a fair share of the work for the Martins.

However, St John's was to face its most devastating disaster on December 10, 1894. On that day the Union and Commercial Banks went broke. The day is known as "Black Monday" in Newfoundland history. James Martin had all his savings wiped out in that bank crash. He and many other citizens were bankrupt because of the terrible financial collapse of the two Newfoundland Banks. James Martin sought and obtained employment with a shipping firm. His son Harry found work with a Marine Engineering Works. It was with this firm that he became interested in the automobile branch of the mechanical trade. After the year 1898 in which the SS *Greenland* went down at the icefields with a loss of 34 lives, Harry's father accepted employment with a shipping firm in Montreal when a former manager, who had moved to that city, offered him a position.

Mrs. Martin and most of the younger members of the family moved with Mr. Martin.

If ever a family had the so-called germ of longevity, the Martins certainly found it. That family lived long beyond the biblical allotted span to man of three score ten years. Very few of the Martin clan have not lived beyond a span of 60 years. Harry Martin married Mary Barton in the year 1905. Mrs. Martin died in the year 1940. By this marriage there were eight children, of which seven are living either in St. John's or Montreal. Harry Martin has two brothers still living. Mike resides in California. He is 100 years of age. His brother, Jack, lives in Holyrood and he is now 98 years of age. James Martin, Harry's, Mike's and Jack's father, lived to be 101 years of age. Their mother died at the age of 99 years. Henry Martin, their grandfather, was 94 years of age when he died, and great grandfather John Martin went to his eternal reward at 92 years.

John Martin (great-grandfather) came out to St. John's as a shipwright to service either his uncle's or cousin's ships. The relative Martin had a fishing and shipping business operating out of St. John's in the late 1700s. John Martin's two sons were boatbuilders and repairers of ships, but Henry became a sea captain and sealing skipper. Harry is named after his grandfather.

A story is told of an incident in Harry Martin's early manhood days. It appears that Harry and one of his chums got employment on a ship sailing out of St. John's on a regular service to Halifax, Boston and New York in or about the year 1898. Harry signed on as an engine room assistant while his friend, Gordy Miller, was signed on as a deckhand. The two men were walking along Duckworth Street, on their way to the pier with their duffle bags slung over their shoulders, when they met a pal of theirs. This "buddy," Stevie Brien by name, asked them where they were going at the hour of 9:00 A.M. They told him they were sailing for Boston at 10:30 A.M. as they were now seamen. Stevie, who had a milk jug in his hand, said, "Wait fellows, I'll go with you."

The two new seamen tried to tell him that they were not passengers. They were seamen. Stevie walked to a nearby doorway and there put the milk jug under the wooden steps that led up to the door. He then followed his buddies up to the wharf where their ship was "docked" or "tied up." Stevie, somehow, got past the "gangway guard" and found a hiding place on board the ship. That night his hiding place was discovered, and Brien was taken to the captain. His two "buddies" came to his rescue, but the captain assigned him to the galley, a duty he had to carry out until the ship returned to St. John's. However, he was allowed to go ashore in all the foreign ports, but had to be escorted by either Martin or Miller and one of the ship's officers.

When the ship docked at St. John's, the three companions disembarked. Miller said to Brien, "Stevie, what are you going to say to your mother when you go home?" Martin said, "It's been almost a month since she sent you for that jug of milk." While Harry and Gordy decided that they would accompany their pal to his home and try to help him get over the expected difficult meeting with his mother, Stevie retrieved the milk jug from under the steps where he had put it about a month earlier. He went into a shop, purchased a fill, and the three friends walked over the hill to Brien's home. When they got there, Stevie said to his mother, "Here's your jug of milk, Mom. Sorry I was a bit late getting it to you." Mrs. Brien told the young men she had a feeling her son had "stowed away," as he often did it during the sealing seasons, and for that reason she was not too worried about him.

Another story told of Harry and his buddies at an earlier time (when he was 13 years old) was an event that took place at

"The Day of the Races." Harry and some of his friends were "down to the pond" to enjoy the fun. They were at the site of the "Greasy Pig Arena" (a compound of about 400 square feet), where a pig of about eight months' growth was greased and let loose. Anyone who thought he could catch the young animal paid his 20 cents and got into the fenced-off arena to try for the prize. The boys were in the "front row" and were enjoying the spectacle of man versus beast. Their laughter must have irked the huge man in the ring doing combat with the pig, because he came over to where they were standing. He is supposed to have said, "So you think you can do better than me. Well, let's see you, young fellow, catch that pig." He picked up Harry, who happened to be nearest, and stood him in the ring. Getting out he said, "Go ahead, laddie, the pig is all yours."

At first Harry was motionless, but the crowd soon began to urge him into action. Harry noticed an old coat on the ground (probably that of an earlier person who had tried for the prize) so he picked it up and threw it over the pig's head. The poor animal was now in the dark, and trying to find daylight. It poked its head out a sleeve of the jacket. Harry held on for dear life, for he now had the pig under his control. With the body of the jacket, he wrapped up the pig with it. By doing so he did not get covered by the grease in which the animal had been coated, and, holding the trussed-up pig, he held on for the required time period. However, the judge of the show would not award the young lad the prize on the grounds that his method of capture was not according to the accepted rules. When the crowd heard the verdict, they pushed forward to the judge, and in no time he reversed his decision. Someone gave Harry a piece of rope and he left the compound with his prize. That Christmas the Martins had roast pork on their table as well as the turkey and plum pudding and other goodies that were extra treats at that time.

Harry Martin was a very good motor mechanic, and an excellent chauffeur. He was hired by one of the Bowring's to drive their "Stanley Steamer," a very famous motor car of that era (early 1900s). At another time he was hired by Reid's as a chauffeur to drive a Stanley Steamer and a Rolls Royce for that family. Later in the 1920s, he drove Mr. Charles Marshall, of Marshall Brothers Ltd. That motor car was a "Cunningham," believed to be one of the first front-wheel drive cars ever made. He drove Dr. Rendell, but the transportation was horse-drawn. It was a wintertime vehicle, a closed-in sleigh. The carriage was a landau on runners, and the interior was heated by a series of hot bricks wrapped in burlap and covered with a rug. When the Rendell's moved to England, the doctor offered the horses to Harry, but stabling and feed for the animals were too expensive and he turned down the offer.

For a while Harry drove for the Herders, owners of *The Evening Telegram*. However, the most famous Newfoundlander for whom he acted as chauffeur was Sir Richard Squires when he was the Prime Minister of Newfoundland. After that service he moved to the Newfoundland Highroads Deptartment as a chauffeur for the Superintendent of Bridges Construction. Here he spent the last 30 years of his working days. Mr. Wm. Whelan, the superintendent, would have no other driver to take him on his rounds of the Avalon Peninsula. It was while driving for this gentleman that Harry told one of his great experiences of the hazards of road construction and bridge building.

On a fine summer's day Harry was summoned to the main office to take Mr. Robinson, Engineer with the Department, and Mr. Whelan to a proposed bridge site near the village of St. Mary's, St. Mary's Bay. When they got to the area where the bridge was to be built, the roads construction crew had everything ripped out and no vehicle could get through to the river.

There was a small lane that had been made by horse-cart traffic that would take them to the river's edge, but it would be rough driving as heavy brush and trees lined both sides of this path. Mr. Robinson was most anxious to see the bridge site so he gave the order to drive over the narrow path. Harry started out on a short drive through what was to be two miles of the darkest woods he had ever seen, and the trees got bigger while the path narrowed to about the width of the vehicle he was driving at the time.

Suddenly they came to the river. It was 30 feet below a sheer cliff. All three got out and had to squeeze between the side of the car and the trees in order to get to the edge of the cliff in front of the stopped vehicle. The engineer and the superintendent looked over the flow of the river below, and having spent some time in technical discussion, they pushed their way back to the side of the car and slowly walked back over the path towards the roads-construction crew. Harry was left to get the vehicle back as best he could and on his own.

His first act was to cut down a few trees. From one he cut two logs of about three feet in length and approximately ten inches in diameter. He used the two logs as wheel chocks. He then "jacked up" the front wheels so that he had a clearance of about 15 inches between wheels and ground. He then pushed the car to the left until it fell off the "jack." He repeated this action many times over the next two hours, however, he had to adjust the rear wheel blockings, and in limbing out or cutting down several trees during that time. By this method he had turned the car a full 180 degrees without any damage to the vehicle. He removed the wheel blocks, got behind the steering wheel and drove back over the narrow path to the newly constructed site where he stopped to let Mr. Robinson and Mr. Whelan get in, and from there back to St. John's over the gravel highways.

The above stories are just a few of the numerous accounts of the happenings in the life and times of Harry Martin. Volumes of eventful stories could be compiled and printed about old St. John's if it were possible to record Harry Martin's memoirs of over a century's experience.

Henry (Harry) Martin resides at 28 William Street and is now confined to his bed. He is wonderfully well cared for by his daughter-in-law, the former Patricia Hynes of Portugal Cove, who is the wife of Harry's youngest son, Leslie. The Leslie Martins have 12 children.

XV

The Dutch Painter of Georgestown

There came to St. John's, in or about the year 1850, a young Dutchman, Peter William Stephinsyn, by name. The young man was bound for New York, but the story has it he was sidetracked to Newfoundland at the requests of his uncles back in Holland. Having heard of their nephew's plans to travel west to the New World, they pleaded with him to stop off at St. John's and from there to go to a small settlement named Renews. The importance of the visit to the Southern Shore Renews community was that at an earlier date their eldest brother had lost his life in a shipwreck and his body along with many others was buried at that place. They collected a considerable sum of money between them and gave it to young Peter to help offset the expenses while in St. John's and travelling to and from Renews. Their request was that he find a suitable stone in Renews, cut a grave marker and inscribe all the details of the late brother and the date of his untimely death. He had to locate the burial site and thereon erect the headstone of his own making on the relative's grave.

Young Stephinsyn was a painter and sculptor who was immigrating to New York to seek his fame and fortune in the New World and in a land of opportunity. His sailing plans now had to be changed so that he could stop off at St. John's. He left Amsterdam and sailed to London, England, and from there he sailed to Waterford, Ireland, where he booked passage to St. John's, arriving here in June in or about the year 1850.

The young painter took lodging at the boarding house of Miss Maloney, then considered one of the most fashionable rooming establishments in St. John's. The Maloney boarding house was located on Cathedral Lane in Tubridstown, the small compact community in Georgestown area of old St. John's.

The following day (after he settled in at his boarding house) Peter Stephinsyn toured the town. The purpose of this walk through the city was to meet with the wealthy merchants, the clergy and the builders in hopes of obtaining interior development work. He also inquired from the businessmen how he could obtain transportation to the settlement of Renews, about accommodations while there, and how long he would have to wait for return transportation. Peter was heading back to his boarding house when a man, sent by a Mr. Peter Gallagher, caught up to him and told him that Mr. Gallagher wanted to talk with him at 3:00 P.M. if he could arrange such a meeting. Stephinsyn agreed, and went back with the messenger to Mr. Gallagher's place of business, arriving there about 3:00 P.M.

Mr. Gallagher had just completed the construction of a large house which he referred to as his cottage. Gallagher had heard from a business associate of a young Dutch painter in town that morning, and was most anxious to have his new house interior decorated before his wife and family arrived from Ireland, so that they could have a big formal opening on the occasion of his family reunion. Peter (the young artist) lost no time in producing his credentials, and was given the job of decorating the mansion with orders to start the following morning.

Mr. Gallagher insisted that the living room was to have a mural depicting St. Patrick driving the snakes out of Ireland, and the dining room mural was to display the miracle of the five loaves and the two fishes. Mrs. Walshe, a widow, his housekeeper would show the young painter around and provide him with information and materials and help as he needed it. All other decorating and painting would be up to the artist's discretion but Mrs. Walshe would be a sort of advisor for Mr. Gallagher in his absence.

Now the young Dutchman had no idea what St. Patrick looked like, so he asked the housekeeper (Mrs. Anne Walshe) to get him a picture of the great Irish Saint. In the meantime Peter had base-painted the walls which were plastered throughout the house. About two days later Mrs. Walshe produced a picture of the Saint driving out the snakes. The picture showed St. Patrick in full Bishop vestments and crosier in hand. At first Peter was astounded, but being a true artist, he soon had the basic strokes marked on the wall. His scale and perspective were such that from any position in the room the painting was most appealing to the eye of the viewer. It took nearly a week to finish the work of art, with all the minor details. When Mr. Gallagher saw the finished product, he was so pleased that he requested Peter to finish the entire interior of the house. The upper floor rooms had to be papered and painted to the tastes of the owner, but in the long run the artist made the changes he wanted to make in all the decorating of the mansion. Gallagher changed his mind for the din-

ing room and the mural was now "The Wedding Feast of Cana."
Peter, once again, asked Mrs. Walshe for help in getting a picture
of this biblical scene. She produced a picture from an old bible
that had been in her family for years.

All these weeks Peter was having his meals in the
Gallagher's house, and Mrs. Walshe was always his only com-
panion during the day. The decorating work had stretched into
six weeks and was now nearing completion. The family was due
to arrive in St. John's about late July, so Mr. Gallagher was most
anxious that all would be completed within the seventh week, so
Peter was asked to live in during this final week. Peter accepted
and moved out of his boarding house that day. He finished up by
Friday and made arrangements to go to Renews the next day.

The only transportation available to Renews was by a
small schooner that sailed from St. John's at noon on Sunday and
Peter took it. He slept on board Saturday night and was away
with the tide the next day. After an uneventful voyage they
arrived in Renews late Sunday evening. The skipper of the
schooner gave Peter lodgings that night and the next day he
went about the business of trying to locate the grave of his relative. Peter stayed in Renews for over a month. It is believed that
he also looked in the burial grounds in Cappahaden and
Ferryland. It is not known if the uncle or great uncle was on his
father's or mother's side of the family. It appears that he had no
success with his search; however, in an old burial ground in
Renews there is what remains of an old headstone that could
have been carved by an artistic stone cutter, but if there had been
any inscription cut in the stone, it has been erased by time and
weather.

Peter returned to St. John's in late September, having chosen a land journey back from Renews. He is known to have
stopped off at Bay Bulls to emboss a headstone in the old Church

of England Cemetery there, and also to decorate a small church while there. When he did arrive in St. John's, he visited the Gallagher residence to see Mrs. Walshe in particular, and to seek work through Mr. Gallagher who was known to have recommended him to some of his wealthy friends who were interested in decorating their mansions. He did get a few small painting and decorating jobs but by November he was looking for work of any kind as all his funds had been used up. He had now fallen in love with Mrs. Walshe.

They were married on November 30, and lived with Mrs. Walshe's daughter, who was married to an American, George Tillman, Jr., who was representing a New York firm doing business in St. John's. Their residence was on Mullock Street (then known as James Street) in Georgestown. The Tillman's moved to New York when the firm recalled Mr. Tillman to take a new position in their head office. They moved in or about the year 1853. The residence on Mullock Street was too big for the Stephinsyns so they rented a small house on Catherine Street. Here Mrs. Stephinsyn opened a small Tuck Shop to help augment the small earnings that Peter was making in the decorating and painting jobs that he could find in St. John's. Work in his profession was very scarce so he had to take house-painting jobs or stone-cutting or engraving headstones, which gave him more income than his artistic decorating.

One day Peter was walking past a group of men who were engaged in the repair of a high house, the end house in a range of three; the building was three stories high. They had a ladder up against the wall that was too short to reach the eave by approximately three feet. The man who had to go to the roof to apply a coat of tar to the felt-covered flat surface was refusing to go up until they could find a ladder that would be, at least, two feet higher than the eave. The foreman on the job was trying to get one of the other men in the crew to go aloft, but they also refused because of the dangerous conditions with the short ladder. Peter, who was a very quiet man, offered to go up and do the job if the foreman would give him some "Dutch Courage." Apparently "Dutch Courage" was a favourite brand of rum that most public houses served their patrons in the St. John's of the 1850s. Peter was not one for heights but the false spirit being aroused with the aid of a noggin of rum erased whatever fears Peter had with regard to height on that day.

Peter tied a rope around his waist, and started up the ladder, trailing the rope as he climbed to the end of the ladder. When he got to the second- or third-last rung, he reached up to the eave and pulled himself upon the roof. He then pulled up the tub or cask of tar and mop with which to apply the waterproof coating. He untied the rope from around his waist and tied it to the chimney, and began his work.

As the day wore on the liquor wore off, and Peter's fear of heights returned when he was nearing the completion of his work. He looked over the edge of the roof, saw the position of the ladder and the group of workers down below. He tried to use the rope which he had tied to the chimney to lower himself to the ladder, but when he stood on the edge of the roof his nerve failed him, and he quickly returned to a safe distance from the edge. The foreman could see the problem of getting his new man off the roof before nightfall, and it was now getting late in the day. Adding to his worries of the man on the roof, a huge crowd had gathered on the street. At about 6:00 P.M. a gentleman (a Scotsman who was one of the towns prominent merchants) came along and inquired into the matter of a gathering of so many people. He was told that there was a man on the roof and they could not get him down. The Scotsman asked how he got up there. When the foreman told them that they had to give him liquor to go up, the Scotsman replied, "Well mon give him a dram and get him down before he falls off." The foreman got one of his crew to go to the nearest tavern to get some liquor. While he was gone, Peter was contacted by loud shouting, to lower the rope. When the messenger returned with the bottle of spirits it was put into a bucket and Peter was signalled to "pull up."

Peter drank the contents of the small container and shortly thereafter, the mop, followed by the bucket and then the tar cask, came over the roof in rapid fashion. The gathering of people on the street quickly dashed for cover, but stayed close enough to see what the man on the roof would do next. They did not have to wait long, for Peter, using the rope and the chimney, lowered himself to the ladder. Having descended about four rungs he let go the rope and came down the ladder to the street level, trailing the rope behind him.

That year Peter's luck changed. He got several interior decorating jobs which kept him steadily employed in his true profession. He was working late one day in October and his wife brought him a lunch at about 10:30 P.M. It was a wet cold night and the distance was considerable. Mrs. Stephinsyn caught cold, and was confined to bed for quite a while. She got up to prepare her husband's dinner for his return but that night her condition got worse. Peter called a doctor but her cold had turned into pneumonia and she died within two weeks. Peter had contacted his wife's daughter, who came from New York to see her mother. She arrived just two days before Mrs. Stephinsyn died.

After the funeral and all the matters were cleaned away Mrs. Tillman waited until Peter had finished the painting and decorating he was engaged to do. She then asked Peter to go to New York with her. Peter accepted and stayed with the Tillmans in New York until he could get established with his profession in that city. Peter died in or about the year 1875.

Regarding his buried relative in Renews, the reason for his visit to St. John's and Newfoundland, no evidence of his erecting a headstone to the uncle can be found today.

XVI

The Conspiracy That Failed

The closing years of the eighteenth century, with regard to Newfoundland, were troubled times. The Act of Union between Ireland and Great Britain, and the rebellion in the south of Ireland that followed extended to St. John's and most of the settlements on the Avalon Peninsula. The larger portion of the population in Newfoundland were immigrants, or of Irish descent, and seemed to support the cause of the United Irishmen in opposing the Union with Britain. In St. John's the people spoke openly of the Act and their resentment towards it. There were many Irishmen, soldiers and sailors stationed in the military garrisons and the men-of-war ships anchored in the harbour, and most of them were not too happy with the Act. They added greatly to the number of settlers of the town with a population of little over 3,600 residents, and to this mood of popular opinion.

The Irish resentment in St. John's had grown to such proportions that about August month, 1799, two United Irishmen came from Dublin, by way of Waterford, to St. John's. They were, it was said, sent out to organize a local branch of the Association, mainly to agitate but to raise recruits and funds to join the uprising in Ireland. One of the organizers was a Phenius Barton (believed to be an alias), a notorious Irish Nationalist. He enlisted in the Royal Newfoundland Regiment, using the name Patrick William Murphy. It was the easiest military service to join as it was made up of local men, most of whom had little or no education. Having been duly sworn in, "Murphy" lost no time in gathering a band of fellow soldiers (of Irish extraction) to whom he administered the United Oath. The other man, whose name was given as Duncan Kerr (no doubt it was also an alias), worked on the civilian townspeople. They were, for the most part, of the labouring class.

He also recruited some fishermen, and all took the United Oath. Nearly all were descendants of, or immigrants from, Ireland. Kerr was instrumental in obtaining about 200 men in support of his cause. From that number he picked seven men to form his Select Party. He made this move so that at no time would there be more than eight men gathered together that could arouse suspicion of a subversive meeting. The "Selects" would confer, after a meeting with "Pockets" of the mass of the recruited Irish Unionists. These "Pockets" never numbered more than eight men, so the "Selects" were spending much time with group meetings and as a result only about 50 men were informed of impending action. No doubt, larger numbers per "Pocket" would have aroused suspicion even by the tavern- and innkeepers of the establishments the labouring class usually frequented every evening.

Murphy, being a bold and fairly well-educated man, made friends with a seaman, Parker by name, of the HMS *Latona*, which was stationed in St. John's Harbour. He soon recruited Parker and several companions who were also sailors on the HMS *Latona*. They too took the United Oath, and formed an integral part of a plan for rebellion and mutiny to support the vote in Ireland. Parker became a key figure in Murphy's planned rebellion. He recruited more sailors on board the *Latona* and administered the United Oath on shipboard. However, he, like Murphy, only solicited Irishmen to the ranks of the conspirators as it appeared that they would be more loyal to support the cause against the Union of Ireland and Britain.

Kerr's meetings with his "Selects" were always held in the open countryside, either on the "Barrens" outside of Fort Townshend or on the banks of Upper Long Pond. He usually conducted the meetings at sunset and at breakup the men were instructed to return to town in pairs or singly, but never in a group. This pattern, he figured, would prevent a betrayal of their actions. He was openly disappointed that the "Selects" could not see more of the "Pockets" (as they were called) of the recruits, but he was pleased with the support and the little funds that were collected for the cause. He had planned to add to the number of "Selects"but this was not possible because of the severe weather of winter and early March of 1800. He had talked the idea over with Murphy but because of the prearranged revolt date both men decided against the addition of "Selects." Murphy would get soldiers at Fort Townshend to join and to take the United Oath, as he had recruited members from Fort William who were willing to help him, by visiting with the soldiers at Townshend. Parker had done all his recruiting on the HMS *Latona* and on his next shore leave he was to meet with Murphy and Kerr.

On the night of April 20, 1800, Murphy, Kerr and Parker met at a public house near the King's Beach where they set about the work of their uprising in St. John's. As there were many soldiers present, the three men left the place and walked up the hill to the Military Road that connected Fort William with Fort Townshend. From here they overlooked the town and the harbour and then after a short while walked over the "Barrens." From there they decided on the night of April 24, 1800, at exact-

ly 11:00 P.M., their conspirators should assemble at the Army
Powder Shed. (The old Army Powder Shed was located where
Belvedere Street meets Barnes Road today.) All the military were
to come with their guns and several rounds of ammunition,
while the civilians were to bring arms (if they had any) and
wrecking tools. At the appointed hour a signal shot would be
fired to notify Parker and his mutineers to seize HMS *Latona*.

Orders were to be given to kill anyone who tried to resist.
St. John's was to be plundered and the loot loaded on board the
HMS *Latona*. The rebels were then to burn the town, board the
Latona and all would sail for Ireland. Should the Navy come out
to capture them they had alternative routes planned to take them
to France or the American coast. The party broke up and
returned to their garrison, ship and home. From their respective
abodes they passed the date and hour of the meeting to their
recruits and each made preparations for April 24, 1800.

On the night of April 24, 1800, Col. Skinner was giving a
party at his residence located near Quidi Vidi Lake. Many officers and local merchants were in attendance. In those days such
parties, given by a high-ranking military officer, were guarded
by soldiers from his Regiment, so Col. Skinner's affair was no different. Most of the officers of his regiment and many of the non-
commissioned personnel were in attendance. The company of
guards under direction of a Sergeant patrolled the estate, but
always two were positioned at the main entrance where the Sgt.
announced the arrival of each guest. Col. Skinner's party resulted in a shuffle of soldiers at the garrison to carry out security on
the post of Signal Hill. Some of Murphy's conspirators were
assigned to duty rosters that night. As the result of the reassign-
ment only 29 soldiers of the Royal Newfoundland Regiment
showed up at the old Army Powder Shed between the hour of
9:30 P.M. and 10:30 P.M.

Three of the soldiers, Privates Carey, Howe and Kelly, who were also conspirators, were late in leaving Signal Hill. Private Lavine, who was to accompany Private Carey, was met by the latter, who told him that he did not trust Howe, and was going to get Private Kelly to make sure that the young soldier went along with them. Lavine was told by Carey to go on his own and to tell Murphy that they would join him within the hour. Lavine then left the Hill and headed towards Quidi Vidi Lake where he saw Howe doing duty at the rear of Col. Skinner's residence. He then hurried along his way to the meeting place. When he got there, he called to Murphy. Kerr, who was talking to Murphy, also came to meet the soldier. Lavine told them what had happened, and when he saw Howe doing guard duty, he had an uneasy feeling about Carey's loyalties to the conspiracy.

It was now about 10:30 P.M. Both Murphy and Kerr began to discuss Carey's moves and what actions would be necessary if he, indeed, was a spy planted in their midst. Just then Kelly appeared, alone, equipped with his rifle and a supply of ammunition. Murphy told Kerr to take Kelly and to flee to the woods. He then told the gathering that he had had word that their plot had been betrayed even to the place of assembly. While he was speaking to the conspirators, the general alarm had sounded at Fort William and Fort Townshend. He told all to flee the site and find safety in the nearby woods. He took Lavine and persuaded him that by heading into town, even in sight of Fort Townshend they would have a better chance of escape.

Within half an hour soldiers from Fort William and Fort Townshend garrisons had converged on the old Army Powder Shed. Here they captured many civilians and only 12 soldiers. Searching parties found one soldier and three civilians hiding in McKie's Grove by dawn of the next day. All the rest had vanished in the darkness. Murphy and Lavine hid in a Fort Townshend wood-storage yard known as the Williams Plantation. It was as Murphy had said, for of all places most unlikely for search by the military was, indeed, in the shadow of the garrison. Here the two fugitives stayed until nightfall, when they left and worked their way to the western section of the town where Murphy counted on and got help from Irishmen who made that area of St. John's their home. Later in the year they made their way, with the help of the new Irish immigrants, along the Southern Shore, where they were believed to have boarded an American fishing vessel in October month that took them to Boston, which was then known as the rebel headquarters of the New Republic.

Kelly and Kerr, in company with a few civilians, escaped through the Upper Long Pond region. They pushed on to Conception Bay where they separated from the civilians. The two men decided they should head towards Placentia. Kelly had been there once and figured it would take them about a month of travelling. He had saved his ammunition so they could provide themselves with food. With this plan they set out over the rough trail that would take them to St. Mary's Bay.

Some say that Kelly and Kerr made good their escape, but others contend that they perished in the wilderness. The latter train of reasoning could very well be what actually happened to them, for in the years of the Great Depression of the twentieth century two skeletons were uncovered by relief workmen who were doing a roadway widening on a section of the Salmonier Roadway that was, even then, a long way from any settlement. An old gun barrel and buttons styled to military wear were found near one of the skeletons.

Parker and his mutineers put up a bit of resistance but were soon overpowered by ship's officers and a platoon of marines. It was said that they were about to blow up the *Latona* but some of the mutineers attacked their leaders from within, and thus saved the ship and ended the possibility of a grave disaster from occurring in the harbour.

Parker and his band were taken to shore to face a court-martial along with the 26 soldiers of the Royal Newfoundland Regiment, and were placed in custody at Fort Townshend. Of the 40 charged with mutiny and revolt, or conspiracy to revolt, five, including Parker, were hanged; nine soldiers and a like number of sailors were sent to Halifax to serve out long prison sentences after which they were to leave the land and never set foot in British North America again. The remainder of the military were severely reprimanded and confined to barracks every day after normal duty hours for a period of six months. All leave and privileges were also suspended for the same length of time.

Many of the civilians were released because of their ignorance and lack of education. It was stated that because of their backwardness they were easily swayed by the glib tongue of Murphy and his cohorts. However, several, who were new residents and were from Ireland, were ordered to leave Newfoundland and never to return. Their personal belongings were confiscated and they had only two weeks to leave the Colony.

Carey was exonerated; his actions were considered most loyal to his king and country. He was promoted to the rank of a Junior Officer and transferred to an unknown Regiment outside Newfoundland. He was transported back to England and from there he was given his new posting. This was done so that friends of the convicted mutineers and rebels could not follow him in order to atone for their lost comrades.

Howe was the son of a Presbyterian clergyman who had come to Newfoundland in mid-July of 1799. He had joined the services and had no connection with the conspiracy. It was learned that Carey used his name so that he could use the time to get free from Lavine in order to notify his superior of the place and hour that the attack on St. John's was to take place. Howe was also given a new posting and was shipped back to England on the same boat that Carey sailed from St. John's. It was said that young Howe, who was completely innocent, wanted to stay in St. John's, but the military authorities deemed it wiser to have him posted to a new Regiment far from Newfoundland for his own safety.

All the condemned men were executed on the side of the old Army Powder Shed where they were to begin their attack on the residents of St. John's. It became their burial grounds.

A report written by the Chief Justice, and submitted to the Colonial Office in London later in the year, revealed that more than 85 percent of the inhabitants of St. John's and as many in the various settlements had taken the United Oath. The latter asked that as many as 1,200 troops be added to the military force to uphold law and order in the Colony.

XVII

The Georgestown Lad Who Retired at Age 30

Philip Broke Baylie-Cooke was the grandson of Sir Philip Bowes Vere Broke who on June 1, 1813 captured the *Chesapeake* off Boston in the war with the United States. In that war the Admiral had been so badly wounded that he was retired from active duty and returned to England. Philip's father was also in the Navy, and was assigned to duty in the West Indies station. Young Philip was born at Broke Hall, Suffolk, England in the year 1834. His mother, Elizabeth Broke, married Calvin Henry Baylie-

Cooke in the summer of the year 1821 and had gone out to the West Indies with her husband shortly after his posting to that station. However, when the Admiral retired to his home in the year 1833, his daughter went back to Suffolk with her children to live with and to care for him, as her mother had died several years previously.

Upon the death of Sir Philip in 1841, Mrs. Baylie-Cooke and her family came out to St. John's where her husband, now a captain, had been posted to a tour of duty. Shortly thereafter the captain resigned his "active duty" commission to take charge of a shipping venture in the coastal Labrador waters for a local firm. He had accumulated enough service time to earn a pension, so the position with the firm of Hunt, Roope, Teagle and Co. in charge of their Labrador branch would give him time to look into a land grant supposed to have been given to his late father-in-law by the British Government, as a token of gratitude for his esteemed and distinguished services in the war of 1812 against the United States. It was said that the land grant was in British North America, and most believed it to be in the area of Fort York, Henley Harbour, Labrador. Baylie-Cooke's Labrador headquarters were set up at Henley Harbour and at the site of the now-abandoned Fort York. It was here that Baylie-Cooke built a cottage to house his family just before winter set in. The older sons and daughters had been sent to England to attend schools there, while young Philip, who was always called "Bay" by his family and friends, stayed in Henley Harbour with his parents.

Here Bay learned how to enjoy the sport of heavy snow and the language of the Eskimo from the young children in his play group. Later he learned how to hunt, trap and snare wild game and the art of driving a team of dogs. Bay was a smart lad and was able to master anything that his Eskimo friends could do. Knowing their language, he was able to get business for his father's firm on many occasions. Bay did not want to leave Labrador, so his parents did not send him to school in England. His mother instructed him in the basic rudiments, such as reading and writing and arithmetic. His social graces were never neglected, and he was always pleasant and courteous.

In the year 1853, Captain Baylie-Cooke became ill. His malady was a carry-over from a sickness that he had suffered when in the West Indies. As his condition worsened, he asked his firm to transfer him to St. John's before the winter set in so that he could be near a medical practitioner should his illness worsen. They consented and even located a house on Georgestown Road (now Monkstown Road) where he could take up residence upon arrival in St. John's. The Baylie-Cooke's closed up their cottage in Henley Harbour, but did not sell it. Mrs. Baylie-Cooke engaged one of her husband's hired hands to take care of the property while they were away. They had every intention of returning after the spring break up and to have the cottage ready for their arrival back at Henley Harbour. Captain Baylie-Cooke was none too well, but insisted on working with his firm and went into their offices every day when his doctor permitted him to get up and move around in the month of February. One morning he went to work (February 27, 1854) and collapsed in the main office. A doctor was called and the captain was taken home from there. He had contracted pneumonia and on March 5 he died.

Mrs. Baylie-Cooke had the body taken back to England for burial as he had requested her to do so before he died. Bay accompanied his mother on her sad voyage to England.

Calvin Henry Baylie-Cooke had entered the Navy as a midshipman in the year 1811 and had retired from active duty in the year 1842. He was buried with full military honours in

Andover, Hampshire in his father's family plot there. After the burial Elizabeth and her son Bay went to Suffolk where the children reunited at Broke Hall for the first time in many years. The two older sons, one a naval officer had just returned from a tour of duty in the Indian Ocean, the other attached to a diplomatic office in France, were home to meet them. The two daughters had married, one to a naval officer stationed at Portsmouth, the other, to a successful lawyer living in London.

Bay stayed in Suffolk with his mother for the next two and a half years. He did not like the leisure lifestyle that his mother had hoped he would adjust to within time. In September he told his mother that he wanted to return to St. John's and to go back to Henley Harbour from there. Elizabeth, knowing that her son loved the life he knew in the wilds of Labrador and of the free way of living in St. John's, consented to his wish. She gave him 1,000 pounds to start up whatever business venture he desired to establish in Newfoundland. She saw to it that he was outfitted with the best of clothing for both entertainment and for wilderness wear. When he was ready to sail, she went to Liverpool to see him on his way.

It was while at Liverpool that she told him that her father's land grant was awarded to the old Admiral shortly after his return to Portsmouth, where he received a hero's welcome for the capture of the *Chesapeake* off Boston. She told him that the land grant was for a tract of land in British North America but his father believed it to be in the Labrador area near Henley Harbour, that he took the position with Hunt, Roope, Teagle and Co. in Labrador so that he could locate and work the grant for his wife and family. She said that she did not have the heart to discourage his ambitions, but hoped and prayed that after a few years he would give it up and return to England. She openly expressed the wish that Bay would not look at the grant as a means of a livelihood.

Philip "Bay" Broke Baylie-Cooke arrived in St. John's on October 17, 1856. His Atlantic voyage was uneventful, but it did afford him time to think out his plans for his future in Newfoundland. He decided on going to Henley Harbour as the cottage was still there and he would spend the winter trapping and hunting. The furs would give him a good financial status after the sale of them and he could hire the lads that he grew up with in the community. Shortly after disembarking in St. John's he found accommodations on James Street (now Mullock Street). From here he checked with the government offices to inquire of Admiral Broke's land grant, but without success, and after that he went looking for a vessel along the harbour front to purchase so that he could start a coastal trading business.

He found such a schooner tied up at the premises of Bennett's. The owner was interested in a bigger boat but was offered too little for it in a trade for the bigger vessel that he selected, so he was selling his own at the best possible price. When Bay made his offer the skipper took it, and agreed to sail the boat to whatever port the new owner requested of him as part of the deal. The vessel was a two-masted schooner of 54 tons draught, and he purchased it for 200 pounds sterling. When all the legal documents were completed, Bay provisioned the ship and got a small cargo to take to Henley Harbour. He hired three seamen who had just finished up work and were looking for employment. At sunrise on October 23, 1856, they set sail for Henley Harbour and arrived there without incident just before the end of the month.

On arrival at Henley Harbour, Bay got the surprise of his life. The cottage had been burned to the ground with all its contents that summer. The fairly large storage shed had escaped the flames but it showed the neglect of three years. All his friends had left the community, but his two Eskimo friends, who were brothers, greeted him at the wharf. That night Bay slept on board his vessel and there planned his next move. He arose early next morning and, with the crew and the Eskimo brothers, cleaned up the shed. There was a vat of pitch in the shed which Bay had one of the crewmen use to coat the roof after some repairs had been made to it. He moved some of the supplies off the ship and stowed them in the shed. After a busy day's work they all retired to the ship where Bay outlined his plan for the following two weeks.

The crewmen were to stay on the ship, but during the day hours clear away the rubble at the cottage site and make necessary repairs to the shed. He and the Eskimoes headed out into the wilderness with guns and snares to catch as many rabbits and shoot as many birds and caribou as was possible. They set up a temporary camp about 30 miles inland and spread out from there to begin their hunt. The party returned to Henley Harbour on November 13, 1856, with a huge catch of rabbits, birds and caribou which they loaded on the vessel. At this time of year the meat was frozen in the ship's hold. It was well preserved for travel. While Bay was inland, the skipper was to buy as much dried salted cod fish as would fill the aft hold. If vats of Cod Oil were available, he was to purchase that also. But he had to bargain for all goods and only buy at the lowest prices. He was instructed to inspect all fish before paying for it. The skipper must have been used to fish buying for he had obtained top-quality produce at a most reasonable price, and indeed, he had the hold filled to near capacity when Bay's party returned from the wilderness.

Bay told the Eskimo brothers to check the trap lines regularly all winter. He gave them keys to the shed where he had stored ample food supplies and gear to carry out their work. He gave them good wages and promised them a small payment for each cured and cleaned pelt, when he returned in the spring. The ship was set to sail on the morning of November 17, 1856, and when they cast off, Bay waved a farewell to the two brothers, speaking to them in their natural tongue. With favourable winds the ship arrived in St. John's by November 25, 1856, without incident. They did stop at several harbours to take on fresh water and purchase vats of cod oil which were carried on deck as the holds were full.

In St. John's the crew and Bay stayed on board overnight but next morning they went ashore. One man stayed to guard the cargo. Bay visited some of the merchants of the town and sold all of his rabbits, birds and caribou meat before noon. The salted fish and oil cargo was sold to Bennett's and offloaded at their premises. The trip netted more than 2,800 pounds sterling in value. He was requested for more produce if and when he could provide it. Bay went into the first Attorney at Law office he saw (it was that of a Mr. Emerson) on his way to the bank to enquire if any houses were on sale. Mr. Emerson said that he had a house on James Street (now Mullock Street) that was up for lease that he could move into immediately, but if it was for outright purchase, he would see what he could do for him.

Bay took the lease until a place was available for purchase. He furnished it and moved in that day. He had the place completely redecorated by December 15, 1856. From here he operated his business, mostly with parties and entertainment for his clients. His ship was moved to the Southside and moored to a wharf owned by a Miller family, who were retired people. They provided a watchman service at an extra fee. Bay spent most of January and February months in the repair of his ship, preparing it for service after the spring breakup. He had built a better cabin in the schooner that would give him more comfort when sailing the Labrador coast. His crewmen's quarters were made more comfortable and a small stove was added to it where clothes could be dried when they were working in inclement weather. One of the crewmen had a "berth" to the seal fishery and asked Bay if he could go. Bay agreed and casually asked if his vessel would be good enough to attempt a trip to the "Ice." The crewman said he thought it a bit risky, but he added, if it was clad with "greenheart," it could well be able to go into the smaller ice floes.

At this time Bay was contemplating installing a steam engine in his vessel, but when he discussed it with a Marine Engineer of one of the Bowring Brothers Ltd. ships, the man told him to get a bigger boat, one that could carry coal and have plenty of room for cargo. Bay dropped that idea and continued to use sail for powering the schooner.

In early May, Bay set out for Henley Harbour and on the way he stopped off at Cape Breton Island where he picked up a load of timber. He was determined to rebuild the cottage at Henley Harbour and make it his summer home. While in Cape Breton Island he met a fur buyer who was on his way north from Boston to collect furs. He asked Bay if he could get passage on his boat, as he had business with a Mr. Cartwright in Labrador. Bay agreed and told him that he had trappers out all winter and was on his way to collect his treated furs which he would sell if the price was right. The buyer was most anxious to do business with Bay and requested to see the merchandise.

When they got to Henley Harbour the two Eskimo brothers greeted Bay with great news of a successful winter's catch. They had beaver, fox, marten, otter and muskrat pelts all cleaned and cured, and the old shed was full with them as well as their own place. Bay showed the buyer the furs, who immediately purchased them on the spot. He hired Bay to take them to St. John's and decided on a trip to Cartwright's premises. Bay could not take him but arranged for a party that was going up the coast to take the buyer with them. The Eskimoes were duly paid, and the boat unloaded.

A start was made on the cottage before Bay headed back to St. John's with his cargo of furs. He had a Bank Promissary Note from the buyer to present to the bank when the furs were delivered to the fur buyers agent in St. John's. After a slow voyage the little vessel arrived in St. John's in mid-June without loss or damage to his valuable cargo. When he showed the furs to the agent in company with the Bank Manager, the payment was made immediately to Bay. The value of the payment was more than 8,500 pounds sterling.

After discharging the furs, and taking on supplies, Bay left port on June 27 and headed back to Henley Harbour. He completed the cottage which he made his summer quarters, and continued his operations there for the next seven years, over which time he was very successful in the fur trade and the salt cod fishery. He stayed in St. John's at his James Street (now Mullock Street) residence during the winter and moved back to Henley Harbour as soon as the ice broke up. However, he soon tired of the rough life of being all the time on the go. He was now a very wealthy young man, and his friends had all left the Newfoundland that he had grown up in.

That winter, 1864, he decided to close out his business. He gave the trapping equipment to the two Eskimo brothers and the boat, which needed repairs, to the crew. He gave the cottage and docking facilities in Henley Harbour to both groups and made arrangements to sail back to England the following spring on the first ship sailing out of St. John's for Liverpool. He spent that winter partying and entertaining. He closed out his lease a week before sailing. He retired to his mother's estate in Suffolk where he lived the life of a country gentleman. As far as is known he never married, and the family estates went to his brothers and sisters.

XVIII

The Georgestown Pilot: Newfoundland's First Aviator

Victor Sydney Bennett, the second son of Sir John and Lady Bennett, was Newfoundland's first aviator. When Sydney graduated from Bishop Feild College in the year 1913, his father sent him to St. Andrews College in Toronto, Canada, to finish up his education with a degree in Commerce. However, while Sydney was attending classes there, war broke out, and at the age of 18 years, he enlisted in the Royal Flying Corps, later to become the Royal Air Force.

After a brief training course in basic flying, Bennett was posted to overseas duty. He was stationed in Northern Great Britain for a short while, where he did coastal reconnaissance duty. Within six months he was transferred to a tour of duty at the front in France where he distinguished himself by mapping the movements of the German Armies advancing on the Belgian Border. His reconnaissance flights were most helpful to the French and Allied Artillery Batteries. His services won him the Croix de Guerre, one of the Republic of France's highest honours for valour. It was while on active duty that Bennett met up with Sydney Cotton, an Australian, and Alan Butler, an Englishman, who were fellow aviators. The two later came to Newfoundland, where the three reunited and embarked on an aviation business venture that had lasting effects upon the growth of our country. When the war ended, Bennett returned to St. John's and took employment at his father's business for a short while.

In the spring of the year 1919, St. John's became the centre of attraction of all the British aircraft manufacturers of that era. Aeroplanes were arriving from Great Britain on every steamship sailing to the city during the months of April and May. The aircraft manufacturing representatives, with their mechanics, riggers and aviators, were all busy searching out suitable sites for runway layouts. Large sums of money were being spent by Sopwith, Handly Page, Martinsyde and Vickers Vimy Aircraft Companies in the quest of the *Daily Mail* prize valued at 10,000 pounds sterling ($50,000) to be given to the aviator or aviators who would be the first to cross the North Atlantic in a non-stop flight.

Fields outside the city were hired, fences removed and runways were graded while eager aviators awaited the chance to test-fly their favourite aeroplanes so that they could beat out their rivals in quest of the fame and fortune that awaited the first to succeed in this great adventure. Sydney Bennett knew them all from his Royal Flying Corps training days and was their most loyal helper in locating the best accommodations available while trying to secure suitable property for runway use at reasonable prices. As Alcock and Brown were the last to arrive, and being good friends of his, he drove many miles of country roads in search of a field large enough for their twin-engined-aeroplane's required long take-off strip.

A Major K.E. Clayton-Kennedy came to St. John's on May 12, 1919, representing the Aircraft Manufacturing Co. of London to present his firm's application to the Newfoundland Government. The Aircraft Manufacturing Co. proposed to operate aerial mail and passenger service for Newfoundland. In their proposal they stressed the fact that local personnel would have employment preferences. They claimed that if the Newfoundland Government acted quickly and approved the application their services would begin within 12 months from date of its approval.

Major Kennedy was to stay in St. John's to await the Government's approval or rejection of their application. While he waited the major made several public appearances in which he greatly advertised the advantages of airmail services and the growth of Newfoundland through air transport. The Government finally approved the Act known as the "Aerial Mail Service Act of 1919," on the fifth day of June, 1919. Kennedy returned to England where he immediately began the work of organizing the movement of equipment to St. John's. He hired engineers to come out to Newfoundland to select runway sites across the island and to chose the headquarters location near the city. Then he turned his attention to the matter of hiring aircraft mechanics, aircraft riggers and aviators. One of the airmen was Sydney Cotton who hired on with his own aeroplane. It was late in November, 1920, when all the pilots, mechanics and aircraft riggers arrived in St. John's. They were met by Sydney Bennett who arranged their hotel accommodations and saw to it that their equipment was properly offloaded at dockside.

All the aircraft activities of the year 1919 aroused the imagination of a young city merchant, a Mr. Bert Job, who had vested interests in the Newfoundland sealing industry. He readily saw the possibilities and advantages over his competitors should he convince this new Aircraft Manufacturing Co. management to hire one of their aeroplanes to fly out over the icefields on the "front" and to spot the main seal herd the following spring (1920). He talked the idea over with two fellow merchants, Eric Bowring and James Baird about the scheme's possibilities. Mr.

Job contended that if aeroplanes could spot submarines which were underwater, it would be much easier to sight seals on the ice floes at the "front" in the spring, which were on the surface. Mr. Job was going to England on business later that year so it was agreed that he visit Major Kennedy and talk the matter over with him. The result was that Major Kennedy entered into a contract to locate seal herds for the Sealing Companies Syndicate at a price of $50,000 in the spring of 1921 with a renewal clause for the following two years. This seal spotting was to take place from two bases, one in St. John's and the other located at Botwood.

Once again Sydney Bennett arranged for the transportation of equipment and supplies of the Aircraft Manufacturing Co. to Botwood. He also advised the party of the best type of clothing for both ground and air crews to wear in northern Newfoundland climate. The party had been in Botwood for more than three weeks and in all that time nothing was done towards the erection of a hangar. They had rented two sheds where all the crews helped on the basic assembly of the aircraft, so that when the hangar was finally built, no time would be wasted with the minor or finishing rigging work.

It was late December and rumours were on the go that all was not well with the company back in St. John's. Major Kennedy was confronted with overdrafts at the bank. His contract with the Sealing Companies Syndicate called for a one-time payment of $50,000. The Major had already spent $26,000 against his shaky contract. The bank officials were more disturbed than the sealing companies. When the bank manager examined the finer points of the contract, he gave Kennedy three days to redeem the overdrafts. He did so on the grounds that no flights had been made out over the icefields to date, and it was now mid-January 1921. Botwood had already had two severe snowstorms and winter was only started. Major Kennedy called Cotton into St. John's on

January 15, 1921, and they both went to a meeting with the Sealing Company Syndicate. After many hours of discussions the Syndicate agreed to honour their commitment, but at a reduced rate and only if Cotton took over the operation. The bank manager, who was at this meeting, agreed with the Syndicate.

When Cotton took over, Major Kennedy, now being out of the company, returned to London on the next steamer. The bank manager agreed to Cotton's new terms simply because he could find no buyers for the aeroplanes and the related equipment. The hangar was built at Botwood, in spite of the severe weather, and completed by February 2, 1921. Cotton asked Sydney Bennett to be his number two pilot. As for seal spotting that year very little was done, and only the few airmail contracts that the companies were able to secure mainly through the efforts of Sydney Bennett, the airline would have been closed down. Cotton went to England in May in hopes of securing new capital with which to rebuild the company and prepare for a better season in 1922 in his seal spotting contract with the Sealing Companies Syndicate.

In London, Cotton went to see his lawyers to whom he explained what had taken place in Newfoundland. He asked them if it were possible to get a new backer so that with the experience of the past winter a better-equipped air service could be in place to locate seal herds in 1922. His lawyers put him on to a Mr. Allan Butler, a young qualified pilot, trained in the Royal Flying Corps, who had just inherited a huge fortune. When Cotton met Butler, being friends in flying school in 1915-1916, they hit it off very well. Butler agreed to back the venture provided he was to have 50 per cent of the share of the company. Cotton agreed and a contract was drawn up and the company now became the Aerial Survey Co. with a capital of 100,000 pounds sterling. Cotton was advanced 8,000 pounds sterling to purchase new aeroplanes for delivery to St. John's that summer. Butler would join Cotton and Bennett later in the year in St. John's.

When Cotton returned to St. John's, he and Bennett went to see the Postmaster with the hope of securing airmail contracts in Northern Newfoundland and having the existing winter runs extended. They were successful in getting a contract to carry mail to Southern Labrador. All the short runs in Northern Newfoundland were renewed for wintertime flights. Butler came to St. John's in September and spent most of his time flying one of the new planes on short runs out of the Botwood base with Sydney Bennett. It was about this time that Cotton managed to sell the management of the Anglo Newfoundland Development Company in Grand Falls a contract to conduct an aerial survey of their timber holdings in Central Newfoundland. Butler and Bennett and their air crews spent a considerable amount of time on this contract. However, Cotton got a call from the Postmaster in St. John's concerning a contract that Bennett and Cotton were seeking to fly an airmail from St. John's to Halifax, N.S. earlier in the year. When Cotton signed this contract, he called Sydney Bennett into St. John's, and within the week they were ready to depart with the first mail of this contract.

The flight was to be made from St. John's to Halifax by way of Botwood and along the railway route to Port aux Basques, across the Cabot Strait and down the shore of Nova Scotia to Halifax. The weather turned bad when the pilots were over Deer Lake and resulted in a crash. Bennett suffered a broken arm while Cotton had a broken leg. Both men were taken to St. John's where they were hospitalized for more than a month. The airmail was placed on a west-bound train and finally delivered to the Halifax Postmaster several days later.

The following spring, Bennett operated a plane out of Botwood to spot seals and drop mail to the sealers of the various ships at the "front." Cotton and Butler operated out of St. John's. They too dropped mail to the ships of the fleet occupying the seal fishery at the "front." It was in this year that Cotton decided that he agree to a settlement with Butler concerning the future of the Airline Company so he decided to talk with Butler about giving him 100 per cent in the Hawkes Bay Trading Co. Ltd., that he and Alan owned equally between them, in exchange for 100 per cent ownership in the Airline. Butler agreed to do this, so a deal was signed between them within the month.

Cotton asked Bennett to stay with the Airline Company and to manage the Northern branch operating out of the Botwood base. The Airline lasted for another year but with no great increase in passenger, mail, and aerial survey work and no improvements in the seal-spotting project. Cotton sold all of the equipment and most of the aeroplanes in Ontario. One Martinsyde plane was sold to the Hawkes Bay Trading Co. Ltd. After all assets were disposed of, Cotton went to New York. Sydney Bennett went to work with Butler's Hawkes Bay Trading Co. Ltd., where he did considerable flying in the interests of that company. Mr. Bennett was later appointed manager and general supervisor of other Butler interests throughout Newfoundland. These included the Marine Agencies Ltd., of which he later became President, and the Reid lands on the Gander and elsewhere in the central districts area of the Island. Sydney Bennett was no longer flying businessmen around the country or taking prospecting parties into the interior. He was now stationed in St. John's from where he directed all the Butler interests in Newfoundland. He was a key figure in the acquisition of some of the Gander timber area sold to the Anglo Nfld. Development Co. (A.N.D. Co.). For his participation, he was later made a director of that company.

Sydney Bennett married Miss Winefride Redmond Browne of London, England in the year 1928. The Sydney Bennetts had three children, a son and two daughters. His son, Victor, resides in Montreal, Quebec where he is president of Inotech Aviation Ltd., which has a branch office and aircraft service and maintenance hangar at St. John's Airport. Victor visits St. John's regularly in connection with aircraft business at his St. John's Airport facilities of which Mr. Jim Collins is the local manager.

Newfoundland's first aviator died on June 4, 1945 at his residence on Monkstown Road in the Georgestown area of St. John's. He was 48 years of age at the time of his death. Mr. Bennett is buried in the family plot of the Church of England Cemetery on Forest Road. His widow resides in Montreal; of their daughters, Trilby lives in the U.S. and Judith is a resident of Windsor, Ontario.

XIX

The Railway Accident in Georgestown

In the year 1880, the Whiteway Government decided to build a Railway from St. John's to Halls Bay. This proposed railway was to provide access to coastal communities and to open up the mineral and forest resources of the Notre Dame Bay area of Newfoundland. Along this railway line at mile 50, a branch railway was to be built to Harbour Grace in order to give freight and passenger services to the north shore of Conception Bay through Harbour Grace.

Early in the year 1881, the Government called for tenders to construct this proposed railway. The bid made by an American Syndicate formed by a Mr. A. Blackman of New York was awarded the contract. The contract was duly signed between the

Newfoundland Government and the Syndicate (Blackman sign-
ing for the Syndicate) on April 20, 1881. By an agreement clause,
the Syndicate was to own the railway after the line's completion
which was to be constructed in five years. The Government, however, held the right to buy back the railway from the Syndicate
after a period of 35 years. Another clause stated that the
Newfoundland Government had to purchase and provide the
land necessary for the railway right-of-way. The Syndicate was to
deposit $100,000 in United States bonds by no later than August
9, 1881 as a guarantee for the completion of their contract within
the specified time agreed upon as stated in this contract.

The bonds for this Newfoundland Railway Company (the
name given by the Syndicate) were raised in England and during
that first summer, materials and equipment began to arrive in St.
John's in preparation for the beginning of the line construction.

The Railway was to run from Fort William in St. John's East
End (the Newfoundland Hotel presently stands on the site of the
first Railway Depot) through the city by a right-of-way that is
today Empire Avenue and part of Blackmarsh Road, thence
through the country back of Donovans, through to Topsail and
points west. That part of the original line this side of Donovans is
no longer part of the Railway right-of-way, and what sections
that are not public roads, have long since grown over with brush
and trees. By the end of the year 1882, the railway line had been
completed as far as Holyrood. In September trains were in operation three days a week giving services to the settlements along
the south shore of Conception Bay. At Holyrood the steamer *Lady
Glover* (named after the Governor's wife) took passengers and
freight to the towns and small settlements along the Conception
Bay North Shore.

In the year 1884, the Newfoundland Railway Company
defaulted and was placed into receivership. A Sir Francis Evans

was appointed to administer and finish the line to Harbour Grace for the bondholders. After a few years these bondholders wanted out, so the Newfoundland Government finally bought out their shares in the year 1897. Shortly before this the government had paid a little more than one and a half million dollars to the Syndicate for complete ownership of the Newfoundland Railway Company from St. John's to Harbour Grace. Now in the year 1888, the Government had constructed a railway from mile 50 to Placentia. They had given the town that grew up around mile 50 the name of Whitbourne in that year. In the following year, the Government called tenders for the building of a railway from mile 56, which was called Placentia Junction, to Halls Bay. The tender of Mr. R.G. Reid was accepted by the Newfoundland Government and all of the agreements were duly signed on June 16, 1890. The work of line construction and station facilities got underway almost immediately in that year. Later contracts with R.G. Reid gave us our railway from St. John's to Port aux Basques.

The start-up of the original line construction began on the morning of August 16, 1881, one week after the arrival of a Mr. James Bolland, Chief Engineer of construction for the American Syndicate. Mr. Bolland came from England. He hired 50 labourers and put them to work at a place which was about 400 feet east of present-day Bonaventure-Empire Avenues intersection. (The place is about opposite the residence of Mr. Harvey Williams on the south side of the Avenue, and Mr. L. Pike's home is to the north side of the commencement site.) The line was started here because the government of the day had difficulty in the purchase of the right-of-way farther east toward Kings Bridge Road. The landowners, for the most part, were against the line construction in the East End because they complained the grade was too steep. They were not against the Railway but wanted it located in the

Riverhead area of the harbour of St. John's because the grade up Waterford Valley was far less than the route chosen from Fort William to Donovans. The land was finally obtained by expropriation and the work progressed in both directions from the site of commencement. The crew working westward had no confrontation with land owners. However, the controversial Mr. Blackman had many quarrels with land owners, some resulting in court cases in which he was fined on several occasions.

On the morning of June 12, 1897, the train under the capable command of Conductor Bartlett left Fort William Depot at 9:00 A.M. It had a large freight and many passengers for points along the route to Holyrood. The engineer, Mr. Fred Glascoe, asked his fireman, John Byrne, to build up a good head of steam because of the heavy load that his engine had to pull over the line up grade from the depot. They were progressing at a steady rate and were about one mile out from the Fort William Depot when the boiler in their locomotive exploded. The engineer was killed instantly and through a miracle, Mr. Byrne was blown out of the cab. He landed in O'Dwyer's Field to the north of the line, more than 100 feet from the scene of the blast, and more than 30 feet below the level of the track. The site of the accident was about 600 feet west of where Carpasian Road crosses Empire Avenue today. The locomotive and tender rolled over the embankment but did not crush Mr. Byrne who was found at the bottom of the slope. At the time Mr. Byrne's wife was expecting their first child, and this evidently was on Mr. Byrne's mind, for when a doctor came to his aid he refused to be taken to the hospital. The doctor attended his badly scalded legs and other cuts that he suffered from the blast. Mr. Byrne was taken to his home on Plymouth Road and without aid walked into the house.

Mr. Byrne was greatly worried that some busybody would run into his house and tell his wife of the terrible explosion that had taken place in Georgestown that morning. His worry was that the shock his wife would get might have adverse effects on their unborn child. (The Byrnes were blessed with a daughter on July 2, 1897.)

Mr. Byrne was later visited by his doctor, and visited the hospital regularly to have his scalded legs and other burns properly dressed. He spent the next 18 months recuperating from his injuries in that accident. He never went back to railroading, but took a job as Boiler Room Operator with Harvey Brehm Butter Factory Ltd. In the winter months he would use "puttees" to wrap around his legs. When these were no longer available, he would use a strong craft paper as wraps to ward off the cold that affected his legs. He retired in the year 1942. Mr. Byrne died December 1, 1946, at the age of 76 years. He is buried in Mt. Carmel Cemetery. Fred Glascoe was 26 years of age and unmarried when he lost his life in the explosion accident of June 12, 1897 on the railroad line that ran through the Georgestown area of St. John's. He is buried in Belvedere Cemetery.

XX

The Barnes Family of Georgestown

Of all the patriotic families of Newfoundland, the Barnes family that settled in the Georgestown area of old St. John's was, in all probability, the most famous.

Richard Barnes, born in Waterford, Ireland in or about the year 1739, migrated to the new world in the year 1756. He first settled in Boston, Massachusetts, New England, where he found work in the shipbuilding trade. He was employed in this industry for about three years, and learned his trade well. He then moved to Halifax, Nova Scotia, in the month of March, 1759, where he found work as a ships repair foreman. The work was mostly in the form of maintenance of ships (schooners) being made ready for the upcoming fishing season. It was while in this employment that Richard Barnes learned of the supply necessities of ships for Newfoundland. As years went by, Richard toyed with the idea of heading to St. John's and in the spring of 1766, he made the move.

In St. John's, Richard Barnes went to work as a fisherman (something he knew nothing about) and stayed with his employer for the next five years. He was able to work all year-round because being a skilled shipwright when the fishing season ended, he plied his trade in ship maintenance and repairs through the winter months. Through his thriftiness and the steady work pattern Richard Barnes was able to save a good portion of his earnings. He had been looking for a small store along the Lower Path (Water Street) to start up a ships supply and provisions business during the late months of the year (1770) and located a place that suited his plans.

In the year 1771, Richard Barnes purchased the small store (the Board of Trade Building now stands upon the site of that store) and started up his business. By way of hard work and long hours he built up a modest business in marine supplies and provisions to the trade. It was during the autumn of the year 1770 when Richard Barnes was visiting a lawyer to start negotiations to buy up the Lower Path property that he first met Katherine Ralph. That meeting led to the relationship that culminated in the marriage of Richard and Katherine in St. John's on January 31, 1772.

The Barneses lived over their store where they both put in long hours and hard work to build up their marine supplies and provisions enterprise. They added a dry goods department and later expanded the business with a general hardware outlet. It was here that all seven children were born. William, their first child, arrived in January, 1773. John was born February 1, 1776. Richard Jr. arrived February 3, 1777. Henry (1) was born August 22, 1778 and died in early September. Another son was born September 7, 1780 and was named Henry (this custom of a child being named the same as an infant who had died shortly after birth was not unusual in that era). Their first daughter was born September 12, 1781 and was named Elizabeth. Ruth came into this world March 24, 1783. Richard Jr., Ruth, Henry (1) and Henry (2) died before the turn of the century (1800).

Richard Barnes applied for a grant of land in the year 1784. He, like many of wealth, began to obtain land on the outskirts of town. The land Richard applied for was that portion north of the Military Road joining Fort Townshend and Fort William and west of the road to the Queen Victoria Hills defenses (later known as the Georgestown Road and today is Monkstown Road). Richard Barnes's grant was for three acres of land adjacent to the east side of the Williams Plantation (today the site of the R.C. Basilica, Palace, and Presentation Convent). Early in the year 1785, this grant was given to Richard Barnes stating it to be used for residence and agricultural purposes and renewable after 21 years. After that date it would be granted forever if used as requested in the first instance.

Richard immediately began the erection of a substantial building which was to be known as the Barnes Cottage. At about the same time Mr. Barnes hired a farmer, just out from County Mayo and whose name was John Power, to cultivate the two and a half back acres. His first task, however, was to fence the property and erect a shed and stable to house a horse, cow and farm utensils. Farmer Power hired a helper named Thomas Carey, a carpenter then residing in the Signal Hill area of the town.

Richard Barnes had obtained his first ship in the year 1784 and in October of that year had shipped a cargo of fish to Pernambuco, Brazil. The ship carried back a full cargo of molasses, rum and sugar. The molasses and some of the sugar and rum were offloaded in St. John's, but in January 1785, the remaining cargo and fish was shipped to Waterford, Ireland. When the ship returned in March month, John Power was one of the passengers coming out to St. John's. It was said that Barnes named his ship *Ballyroyle* after the escape site on the coast of County Waterford, Ireland.

There was a strong belief that Richard Barnes left Ireland in company with his brother, Alan Henry, a John Butler and his cousin Hubert Walters. Richard was believed to have been a lieutenant in the British Army stationed in Waterford who resigned his commission after his tour of duty expired. His brother Alan Henry was a sub-lieutenant in the British Navy. They, like many other young Irishmen serving in the British services at that time, were zealous advocates of Irish independence. Alan Henry was "on leave" and with his brother, they were visiting friends in County Cork.

While they were there, a skirmish broke out between a British platoon on foot and a large gathering of Irish loyalists. The Irish fighting band, after a day-long fight were well in command. However, the following day a second British platoon came to the aid of their beleaguered comrades and routed the rebels. The Barnes brothers in company with John Butler (a close relative of the Duke of Ormande) and his cousin Hubert Walters fled to a place on the Waterford County coast, called Ballyroyle Cove. Here they hid until nightfall and under the cover of darkness rowed out into the Channel in a boat given to them by an Irish loyalist. The following evening they were picked up by a fishing boat and taken to Brest, France. The four men stayed in France for some time, but in June of the year 1756 the Barnes brothers sailed from Brest, France to America. Alan Henry was British Navy-trained and went to sea working out of the Port of Boston. Richard, who was now out of apprenticeship and free to go where he pleased, moved to Halifax, Nova Scotia in the year 1759. Alan Henry stayed in Boston for a short while, but went to Baltimore as second-in-command of a ship plying in the Caribbean trade.

When the American War of Independence broke out, Alan Henry joined the American Navy. He was given command of the frigate *Randolph*. Heading into battle with a British Man-Of-War fire broke out below decks. It quickly spread to the ship's magazine and the resulting explosion killed all hands on board.

John Butler, one of the men to escape with the Barnes brothers, came out to Newfoundland in or about the year 1780. He was said to have taken Lady Fitzgerald (wife of Lord Edward Fitzgerald) out to her parents then living on Fogo Island. Having seen to it that Lady Fitzgerald was with her kinfolk, he and his wife and family settled in Port de Grave.

Richard Barnes died in St. John's in the year 1802. He had built up a successful marine business, and was one of the leading citizens of the town. He was a strict and religious man. He gave freely of his time to his duties in the Congregational Church of which he was a member. He always allied himself with those advocating the right to religious freedom, and lived to see some easing for that cause. His son William Morris Barnes married Margaret Allan, a granddaughter of James Tubrid, who were Roman Catholics, further proving that freedom to which he always supported as one's personal right.

William, the elder son, having now taken over the management, expanded the business. He purchased two more vessels, the *Royal William* and the *Angler*. This boosted the Barnes shipping fleet to three ocean-going and two coastal boats in total.

At the age of 27, William married Hannah Butler, the daughter of John Butler of Port de Grave in the year 1800. William and Hannah had nine children born to them: John Butler Barnes, 1802; Richard, 1805; Hannah, 1807; William Morris, 1809; Charles Henry, 1812; Charles, 1816; Hannah Katherine, 1813; and Ebenezer, 1821. As years went by William expanded the business and his sons entered the company. Richard entered the political field and when Representative Government was granted, he was elected to represent the district of Trinity. His youngest brother, Ebenezer, was elected to represent Bonavista district. Richard was one of the founding fathers of the Native Society and was the first Secretary Treasurer of that association. He died in the year 1846 and is buried in the Anglican Cathedral yard.

William's wife died July 1876 at the age of 91 years. They are both buried in the family plot in the General Protestant Cemetery. Ebenezer married Jesse Brine. Their daughter Hannah operated the Barnes School on Fleming Street. When she married J.B. Mitchell, her sister Sophia took over the directorship of the school. Due to failing health she had to close out the school. The building was later the home of the Avalon Athletic Club.

John Butler Barnes, the eldest son of William and Hannah (Butler) Barnes, was born in the year 1802 (the same year his grandfather Barnes died) and as a young man, sailed on his father's ship, the *Royal William*. At the death of his father, John Butler Barnes became manager of the business. He directed the outfitting of fishermen in the spring and in the autumn he bought from them dried fish and oils. The produce would then be packed and sent to the West Indies, Brazil and other Caribbean countries in which Barnes owned ships. The ships would return with cargoes of produce such as molasses, rum, sugar, cotton, etc. Much of the cargoes would go direct to Waterford, Liverpool and Brest. The firm now became known as J.B. Barnes and Company. John Butler Barnes commissioned a Mr. Newhook of Green Bay to build a barque. It was named *Fleetwood* and was considered to be one of the best sailing ships ever to sail out of St. John's. The *Fleetwood* was the pride of the J.B. Barnes and Company fleet. The fleet now consisted of *Fleetwood, Napier, Flirt, Charles, Undine, Eliza, Margaret, Citana, Circle, Clyde, Catherine, Phantom, Zingara, Royal William,* and *Angler*. The premises on Water Street were destroyed in the fire of 1846. They were rebuilt later in the year, but due to the loss of many vessels and the failure of the fishery over the years, collapsed in the year 1864.

John Butler Barnes never married. He lived in the family homestead on what was to become Barnes Road. After his death in 1884 the estate was sold. The Barnes Cottage later became the Balsam Hotel, and in 1963 it was purchased by the Sisters of Mercy and torn down to make a playground for the junior pupils of their school.

XXI

More About the Barnes Family

The descendants of Richard and Katherine Barnes distinguished themselves in the life of St. John's, in particular, and Newfoundland generally. Many of them were most active in the political, commercial, educational and cultural fields of endeavour of our city and country.

When Richard Barnes died in the year 1802, his son took over the Barnes Ships Supplies and Provisions Business. The first major undertaking by William was to expand the exporting and transportation of dried and salted fish. He purchased two brigs, the *Royal William* and the *Angler*. The ships had been built in Scotland in the year 1824. When the brigs arrived in St. John's, he hired the captains and some of the crews to run the vessels for the remainder of that year. He sent his son, John Butler, as his personal agent on all foreign voyages in the *Angler*. John Butler had spent many years as a sailor and mate in the smaller schooner *Ballyroyle* plying the coastal trade of Newfoundland shortly after he entered his father's business in the year 1818. John Butler later became captain in command of the *Angler* and conducted all business for his father when in foreign ports. William Morris was the Barnes Company representative for the *Royal William*. His position, at first, was "Supercargo," which meant that he was responsible for the ship and cargo when it arrived at its destination. William Morris later became second officer of the *Royal William*, but never commanded the brig.

The two new ships were big barques and strong sailers. Being fast and strong and having business representatives on board to conduct the affairs of selling and arranging for return cargoes, the Barnes Shipping Enterprise made good profits. They could always get ocean freight for Liverpool, New York and many other ports as either vessel could take the homeward-bound cargo, thus leaving the other ship to take goods to any port on the North Atlantic sea-coasts. The Barnes house flag, white and red over red and white in a quarters pattern, became world famous.

In the year 1826, John Butler Barnes left the port of New York on the third day of October bound home for St. John's with a full cargo of provisions for the Barnes firm. (John Butler had taken an ocean freight to New York from Brazil and while there discharging, he purchased a cargo of provisions for his father.) His ship, the *Angler*, was making good passage, but early the next day the winds came up suddenly out of the southeast. Within the span of two hours it had whipped up into a gale of near-hurricane force. By seven o'clock that evening, they were driven onto the beach of Sable Island. The force of the impact snapped off the ship's masts. In falling they formed a sort of bridge from ship to shore. The crew watched their chances and ran along the so-formed bridge and up to the sandy strand of higher ground. They found some shelter and huddled together within a makeshift tent of sail canvas that one of the crew dragged along as he left the doomed vessel. When the wind abated the next day they salvaged most of the foodstuffs of the cargo.

John Butler Barnes ordered his men to take all available sails, ropes, the galley stove and whatever planks and wood that could be used to make shelters and storage tents at the best site from the biting winds on the Island.

Sable Island, from September to May, was completely uninhabited in those years. It was well off the shipping lanes and there was no form of communication, except by letter, and mail only went by ship to overseas destinations. The crewmen of the ill-fated *Angler* were truly stranded on a deserted island.

In St. John's the people had given up all hope for the safety of the crew of the long-overdue *Angler*. The relatives of all crew members went into mourning for their loved ones. Masses and church services were offered up for their safety, or if lost at sea, then for their souls. The Barnes firm saw to it that all the bereaved families were supplied with food and clothing, as well as fuel, all winter. Mrs. Barnes visited the crewmen's families every week after the provisions and other necessities were made in case someone may need medical attention.

Sometime in late May month in the following year, a schooner out of Nova Scotia sailed up to the Sable Islands, their usual summer fishing grounds, to set out their nets and cod traps. The shipwrecked crew saw this vessel and immediately lit a big fire. They made as much noise as they possibly could in order to attract the attention of the fishermen. The schooner crew did not see or hear them and sailed off. About four days later the schooner came into the beach in search of fresh water and it was only then that they saw the shipwrecked crew.

The schooner took the stranded crew to Halifax and from there they got passage back to St. John's, arriving in port on July 17, 1827. There was great joy in the streets of old St. John's. All who were garbed in black soon dressed up in their finest and came out to meet the men who were given up as lost at sea eight months earlier. William and Hannah Barnes were among the first at the wharf to greet the crewmen. Their son, John Butler, was the last of the crewmen to come ashore.

After the death of William Butler in the year 1845, John Butler and William Morris took over the running of the Barnes firm. John Butler, the oldest of the Barnes children, became President and began the reorganization. He renamed the business to J.B. Barnes and Company. William Morris was named General Manager and stayed ashore. The father, William, had left the old Barnes firm to his two sons, as they had gone to work in the business as soon as they had left school. Richard and Ebenezer had entered politics, while their brother Charles had established his own jewellery store. They had very little interest in the Barnes firm. However, John Butler, when he reorganized the company, did make them shareholders, but with only limited voting rights. Richard died suddenly in the year 1846 at the age of 41 years.

As the shipping business grew, it was necessary to increase the size of the fleet. John Butler Barnes expanded the fleet to more than 13 ocean-going brigs. Many captains and crews were hired and the J.B. Barnes and Company firm became one of the largest shipping enterprises in Newfoundland. The flagship and pride of the fleet was the locally built *Fleetwood*. The business was now so big that both John Butler and William Morris had to devote all their time ashore to the running of the company. They hired the best captains and skippers available and always saw to it that their skippers were well informed as to how they wanted their cargoes handled in foreign ports. The two brothers even devised a code of flag signals to transmit orders to the ships should circumstances warrant new information as the vessels were beyond the Narrows of St. John's Harbour.

The captains were so well trusted that each man took pride in his crew and vessel. The captains even vied with one another to secure the most profitable freights from one foreign port to another. All would try to be the first home to St. John's and only bring the best of produce procurable at the time of sailing. John Butler Barnes never married. He lived at Barnes Cottage with his mother. When she died in the year 1878, he kept the family estate and staff going. He had hoped that William Morris and his family would move in, but by that date most of his nephews and nieces were either away at school or were married. John Butler Barnes died February 6, 1884, at the age of 81 years. The family estate known as Barnes Cottage was sold to Sheriff Carter in the year 1888 for an amount of $6,500. William Morris divided the amount equally between the remaining living members of the family.

Ebenezer, the youngest son of William and Hannah Barnes was the member for Bonavista in the first Representative Government of Newfoundland. He and his brother Richard, the member for Trinity, were elected to office. (At that time half of the members were appointed by the Governor and the other half were elected to office.) Richard was keenly interested in the education program of the colony and he presented the first Education Act in Newfoundland. Ebenezer was a strong advocate for Fishery Reform. He was in office through both good and bad years of the fishery and could see that there was a great need for some sort of reform in the industry. Ebenezer married Jessie Brine in or about the year 1849. They had six children: E. William, Sophia, Louisa, Hannah, Jessie and Elizabeth. Hannah, with the aid of her sisters Sophia and Jessie and her mother, founded the Barnes Private School for Youth at Fleming Street in Georgestown. When Hannah married J.B. Mitchell, her sister Sophia took over the management of the Barnes School. Due to failing health Sophia had to close down the school in the year 1909.

Mrs. J.B. Mitchell became a driving force in the Suffragette Movement. Shortly after World War I, she called a meeting of several leading ladies of St. John's which was held at her home (she then resided at Devon Row) to pioneer voting rights for women. This meeting resulted in a campaign that gathered almost two thousand signatures to a petition. This petition was presented in the form of a Bill, to the House of Assembly by Mr. Small and Mr. LeGrow who were elected members. The Bill was turned down almost immediately and the matter considered over. Undaunted, Mrs. Mitchell and her determined associates, Fanny Ryan Flander and Julia Salter Earle kept up the pressure. They held public meetings in the Pitts Memorial Hall, the Casino, the Mechanics Hall and many other buildings that could hold more than 100 people.

Their efforts paid off. The St. John's Municipal Council, in the year 1921, granted votes to women who were property owners. That year three ladies offered themselves as candidates for office on Council. Julia Salter Earle missed being elected by less than 15 votes. The Monroe Government granted women voting rights in the year 1924. In the General Election of the year 1928, Lady Squires became the first female to be elected to the House of Assembly when she won the Twillingate seat. Mrs. Mitchell was also a strong advocate for the foundation of the Society for Protection of Animals (S.P.A.). Although she was not elected to the first committee, in the year 1912 she helped to draw up the regulations for the Society. Mrs. Mitchell, in company with Mrs. Gosling and Mrs. Monroe, devoted much time to the educational branch of the Society. They went to all the schools and colleges in St. John's where they lectured to the students on the matter of cruelty to animals. This work was done as far back as 1914.

Charles, the fourth son of William and Hannah Barnes, opened his watch repair and jewellery store in St. John's. He married Louisa Lombard in or about the year 1846. There were eight children born to Charles and Louisa: Henry, Mary, Anna, Charles, William, Anna Louisa, Richard and Edward. Henry married Mary Atwill in the year 1881. Henry entered his father's business and became one of the best watch repair experts of his day. He is said to have worked on the R.C. Cathedral Clock and most of the big clocks in St. John's. The Henry Barneses had four children. The oldest, Charles (1883-1946), worked for T & M Winter Ltd. Charles married Daisy Parsons of Harbour Grace. They had three children: Maxwell (1909-1929), Boyd (1912-1961) and Hilson (Mrs. G. Regular) resided in Harbour Grace. James Atwill Barnes (1884-1948) was the second son of the Henry Barneses. He worked at Knowlings and later at Bowring's where he was in charge of the Hardware Department. James Atwill married Elizabeth Peach in or about the year 1907. They had three sons: Cyril W., Hugh H., and J. Gordon. All three sons are living in St. John's.

William Morris Barnes, the second son of William and Hannah Barnes, married Margaret Allen in the year 1848. They had seven children: William M. (1850-1934), Ernest Butler (1853), John Henry (1854), Ellen (1856), Alan (1856-1871), Herbert (1859) and Francis (1861-1904).

William Morris Barnes was elected to the House of Assembly for the district of St. John's East in 1861. He became the Minister of Agriculture and Mines in the Cabinet of that Government.

In the year 1861, William Morris Barnes II, the eldest son of William and Margaret Barnes, made his first sea voyage out of St. John's. He was 11 years of age. That trip to Brazil launched him on his career as a seaman that culminated with the rank of a captain certified by the British Government issued in London verifying his ability and competency to command any ship. Although he started out as an apprentice on the J.B. Barnes and Company ship *Phantom* under command of Captain John Morrissey, young William transferred to the *Neptune* captained by Jim Brown.

In the autumn of the year 1861, the J.B. Barnes Company ran into difficulties. The fishery of that year failed, the Company lost two schooners in heavy gales and three of their ocean-going brigs were badly damaged in terrific Atlantic storms resulting in losses of cargoes. The firms had big debts and their creditors wanted payment.

At a meeting called by the creditors, pressure was brought to bear on the J.B. Barnes and Company firm which resulted in the closeout of their shipping enterprise. However, the firm paid back the creditors at the rate of 97 cents to the dollar. It was considered an unusually high rate and many of the townspeople openly expressed the opinion that perhaps the creditors were too hasty in their actions that caused the closure of such a great firm as the J.B. Barnes and Company.

Seaman Barnes then signed on as a member of the crew in the brig *Mary* owned by Job Brothers Ltd. He worked his way up to captain by way of transferring to ocean-going vessels at St. John's, in New York, Liverpool and other foreign ports. William Barnes married Anastasia Frances Murphy of St. John's in the year 1880. They had six children: John, William, Harold, Allan, Joseph and Ida. Mrs. Barnes died in St. John's on July 17, 1912. Ida, the only daughter, had married in the year 1911. She and her husband lived with her mother who had become seriously ill shortly after Ida married. When Mrs. Barnes died, her husband William Morris II decided to quit his position as Customs Officer to take command of a New York ship whose captain had just terminated his contract while the ship was on dry dock in St. John's. Captain Barnes decided to sell his home because his daughter Ida and her husband wanted to go to Montreal to live. Three of the sons also wanted to move to that city and John had gone to Halifax while William had applied for apprentice on a Furness Withy ship. The captain made arrangements for transportation of his children to Montreal, and when his ship was ready, he sailed to New York. He had sold his home and shared the money between his children.

In the year 1914, Captain Barnes sailed from Galveston, Texas to Liverpool. While in Liverpool, World War I broke out. The captain went into the dockside recruiting office and signed up with the British Navy. His son John joined the Royal Newfoundland Regiment and fought in the Dardanelles. He was badly wounded in France. His son William left the Furness Withy ship in New York and joined the U.S. Navy. He rose to the rank of captain by war's end and stayed in the U.S. Navy.

Captain William Morris Barnes, R.N., was torpedoed three times during that war. He was twice torpedoed in the North Atlantic and once in the Adriatic Sea. He was under coastal bombardment off the French Coast and when in command of a Minesweeper he was attacked by a surfaced U-boat. He rammed the sub and the two ships sank. He lost seven of his crew. Seventeen were picked up by a nearby destroyer.

After the war, Captain Barnes returned to New York. He took command of a freighter plying the Caribbean trade and retired in 1928. He resided with his son William on Long Island, where he died in 1934.

His son Harold joined the Canadian Overseas Forces and was killed in France in the summer of 1916.

None of the Barnes descendants live in Georgestown today.

XXII

Captain Cleary: The Plimsoll of Newfoundland

Philip Cleary was born in St. John's on the tenth day of July in the year 1825. He was the second child of Thomas Patrick and Josephine Cleary who migrated from County Waterford, Ireland in or about the year 1820. The Clearys were of good middle-class Irish stock. Mr. Cleary found employment in the cooperage trade, where he rose to foreman in the warehousing department of his employer. The Clearys first settled in the Hoylestown area of St. John's but by 1822 had moved to the Riverhead section of the city. This move was two-fold. Mr. Cleary's place of employment was on the Southside and many Irish families that had lately arrived in St. John's had settled in that area of the old city. The Clearys made one more move, this time to the Theatre Hill section of the town. Here Mr. Cleary became the keeper of the Playhouse Theatre.

Young Philip attended formal school for about seven years. At age 11 he had completed the *Third Book*. (It should be noted that the *Third Book* was not the third reader such as the *McGuppy Readers*, *The Royal Readers*, or the *Christian Brothers Readers* that the schoolchildren used in the lower forms or grades. It referred to the *Third Book of Euclid*, which by today's standards would be equal to or better than Grade X or Grade XI level of education.) Phillip, like many boys of his era, longed for the life of a seaman and the adventures that went with the association of going to sea.

In early summer of the year 1836, young Cleary visited all the shipping firms along the waterfront in search of work at sea. He was successful in "hiring on" as a cabin boy in the *Royal William* owned by the Barnes Shipping Company. The vessel was then under the command of a Captain Brooking, a master mariner out of Greenoch, Scotland. At the time of sailing from St. John's to Brazil, another youth, Angus Frazer by name, who was 15 years of age and a nephew of the captain, joined the crew. The two boys became great friends and helped one another during that voyage. En route to Barbados, their first port of call, the *Royal William* encountered storm after storm. Several of the crew were injured and some were sick. Young Cleary never fell ill to the roll of the ship no matter how rough and stormy the weather.

At Barbados three of the crew had to be put into hospital because of serious injuries. Two others left the vessel. The captain, having observed the seaworthiness off young Cleary, asked the youth if he would like to "article on" as a seaman rather than remain the cabin boy. Before the *Royal William* left port in Barbados, Philip Cleary signed on as a seaman. He was now 12 years old, and thus began his apprenticeship towards his eventual goal of someday becoming a sea captain.

Captain Brooking saw to it that young Cleary was well instructed in all methods of seamanship and in navigational instruments. Every evening, while at sea, the captain would take Philip and his nephew into his cabin and there conduct classes of instructions. On several occasions he would have his first mate take the boys aside during the day and teach them how to use the "lead line" in sounding for depths of water. Never did the lads escape their turns of "deck watch." They were treated the same as the rest of the crew in regard to shipboard duties. When Captain Brooking left the Barnes Shipping Company employ he asked young Cleary to go with him. Philip went with the captain but Angus Frazer stayed with the *Royal William*. He later went to Halifax, and from there moved to the west coast of Canada.

Philip Cleary moved up the ladder of success quickly. He became Captain Brooking's first mate at the age of 23 years. He received his Master Mariners Certificate at age 25 and from the year 1850 onward, he became famous in the maritime history of Newfoundland. Captain Cleary had that burning ambition and great drive to someday own his ship rather than to command vessels for other men. He strove to finance the purchase of a vessel as soon as one became available, one that was in good condition and also big enough to stand up to tropical and northern seas and weather conditions. This he found in New York when he purchased a brig formerly owned by the Barnes Shipping Company.

The *Phantom* was in excellent condition for her age. She was a good sailer and could carry big cargoes. With this ship the rewards of transporting goods to and from foreign ports came at such a rate that after the first investment in the year 1853, Captain Cleary had to get more ships. The captain only hired men to skipper his vessels who had been first mates of his choice in ships that he had commanded for other shipping companies in former days. These men were capable sailors and had been trained in the same style as his seamanship. Also around this time, he took command of a brig owned by Tessier's of St. John's and stayed with that shipping firm for three years. He then went to Liverpool where he captained a steamer working the South Atlantic trade. While in Liverpool awaiting the loading of a cargo, he learned of a steamer that was for sale in Glasgow. It was late summer in the year 1858 when he returned to Liverpool. He immediately went to Glasgow and examined the vessel. It proved to be the type and size that he considered right for his venture, so he arranged finances and sailed his new ship, the *Ariel*, to St. John's, arriving here with a full cargo for firms in the city.

There had been considerable talk about pending legislation to inaugurate a coastal mail service to the settlements of Newfoundland all that year. However, nothing was done during the Fall sitting of the Legislature. Captain Cleary had his eye set on getting this contract, so he kept in close contact with the day-to-day happenings in the House. The captain did his usual shipping to South America and to the United States without fail. In fact his business was getting to the level where he had to increase his fleet or lose much trade. Philip Cleary had married Josephine Forward the year before he purchased the *Ariel* and had moved into a new house that he had built on Monkstown Road. It was here that all of his children were born and lived out their youthful years.

In the year 1860, the fisheries of Newfoundland were almost a complete failure. The government of Prime Minister Kent was in turmoil. A serious conflict broke out between the administration and Bishop Mullock over a proposed contract to carry mail to the coastal settlements. An Act had been passed in which 3,000 pounds sterling a year grant was to be awarded to a local steamship company to carry mail to the coastal settlements of Newfoundland. Bishop Mullock, who had been a most ardent supporter of improved communications for the people of coastal Newfoundland, was in New York. Judge Little was there with him. During their visit to that city they had looked into the possibilities of entering into an agreement of chartering a steamship that gave all the appearances that it would meet the requirements of such a contract to carry out the delivery of mail services to the Newfoundland coastal settlements. They virtually assured the ship owners that the twice-monthly services would be granted that company. When the Kent Government firmly refused to charter this ship, the *Victoria*, the Bishop denounced the Administration. The *Victoria* was eventually put into service locally, but not on contract to carry the mails. She was found to be unsuited to perform the services for which she was now hired to carry out.

In September of the year 1861, the *Victoria* was returned to New York. (It is interesting to note that another mail packet [ship] of the same name plied the Conception service routes in the year 1850. That *Victoria* was owned and operated by a Mr. E. Phelan of Carbonear. On September 9, 1850, a severe storm broke over the Avalon Peninsula. The *Victoria* had sailed out of St. John's at about 11:00 A.M. As the day advanced, the storm worsened. Once outside The Narrows, the ship was caught up in the strong winds and heavy seas. It was last sighted off Cape St. Francis. That *Victoria* with all on board was never seen again.)

In the year 1863, a Mail Carrying Contract was awarded to deliver mail to the Coastal Settlements of Newfoundland. The successful bidder was Captain Cleary. This mail service started on the twenty-first of May in that year. It was the first official mail contract to be let by the Newfoundland Government to service coastal settlements by steamer. The life of this contract lasted seven years. In the year 1870, Captain Cleary passed over command of his ship, SS *Ariel*, to a Captain Hogan who carried out his duties in a most capable manner. The *Ariel* was replaced by the *Tiger* and *Leopard* that year. Captain Cleary used one to service the South Coast Settlements and the other to take mails to the North Coast Settlements. He sold the *Ariel* to a Captain Sopp in the year 1870. Five years later the vessel was lost at Red Bay in the Strait of Belle Isle. Her gallant captain and two of his crew went down in the *Ariel*.

In 1872, Captain Cleary sold all his interest in his shipping enterprise to his fleet commodore, Captain Hogan, and retired from maritime activities. He now turned all his energies and resources to the mining activities of Newfoundland. In the mining venture he put much needed money and time into the development of the copper finds in the northern bays of the island. He then spent considerable time on the west coast prospecting for minerals of all kinds. His search resulted in uncovering asbestos and gypsum in the Port au Port area. Philip Cleary became keenly interested in the St. Georges Coal Fields. Here he prospected and invested the money for the drilling of bore holes to determine the extent of his coal claim.

The Cleary seam gave all the appearances of being a high-grade steam coal. The coal vein was from three to four feet in depth. The length of the seam was never fully examined, but as it extended from the Crabbes River to the Middle Barachois Brook it was estimated to be approximately more than three miles. Captain Cleary had slight investments in the Silver Cliff mines of Placentia Bay, but at this time he had been appointed to the Legislature Council, where he had recently turned his abilities and efforts to make better protective laws to safeguard the "men who go down to the sea in ships." His efforts to have new protective laws and measures for seamen and fisherfolk earned him the popular title "Plimsoll Cleary." Even the news media referred to him as "The Plimsoll of Newfoundland." Full credit was given to Captain Cleary for having a Lloyds Surveyor appointment whose duty it was to examine all vessels prosecuting the fishery of the country.

When the Simpson Company of New York began the building of the Dry Dock in the year 1881, they hired Captain Cleary as their superintendent to oversee the construction through to the finish. When the project was completed he then became the manager of the facility in which post he carried out his duties in a most efficient and capable manner. He returned from New York in the year 1896, and shortly thereafter his health failed. He spent the next 11 years as a near-invalid at his home on Monkstown Road where he died April 19, 1907.

Captain Cleary was twice married. His second wife was the former Miss Catherine Nugent. Of his children: George moved to the city of New York, Philip worked with the Reid Nfld. Co. and later with the Newfoundland Railway, John V. became a professor at Fordham University in New York, Vincent worked at the Bank of Montreal, and his daughter Josephine resided with Mrs. Cleary at the Cleary home on Monkstown Road. Josephine was a registered nurse. After the death of Mrs. Cleary she later married Mr. George Kearney. Mrs. Kearney died about two years ago.

XXIII

The Famous Mitchell's Gardens

Ever since the year 1583, St. John's has been known to have had a "Garden" of great prominence. Edward Hayes, captain of the *Golden Hind*, the only surviving ship of Sir Humphrey

Gilbert's little fleet to return safely to England, stated in his official report that on Sunday, August 4, 1583:

> Sir Humphrey and his Officers were
> brought on land by the English Merchants who
> showed them a place for walks and picnicking
> they call "The Garden." The place having been
> formed by Nature rather than by the work of
> man. Wild flowers and wild raspberries grow in
> abundance alongside the paths on the banks of
> the Burn. The inhabitants of the Town frequent
> this "Garden" on Sundays for walks and family
> partying. The young children play there, under
> the guidance of female servants on other days ...

Cartographer Thornton's map (1670) of early St. John's
shows seven plantations, all bordering on the northern side of
the harbourfront. They were spaced at intervals from Maggoty
Cove in the East to the Riverhead (Waterford River) in the West.
The spacing between the large Plantations (it is stated), were
reserved as "Ship's Rooms" for the migratory fishing fleets.

The first permanent resident of St. John's is believed to
have been a Mr. Thomas Oxford who was closely followed by a
Mr. John Downing. They are said to have settled here in or about
1603. However, they and the other planters had great difficulty in
holding their properties. Their adversaries were the West
Country Merchants. The West Country Merchants had great and
powerful influence with the ruling government in London. They
wanted Newfoundland for their sole fishing interests and advo-
cated complete cancellation of all property rights in the Island.
The struggle went on indefinitely until in the year 1675, the most
successful resident and citizen of St. John's at that time, with the

aid of Sir John Berry, won the rights of the settlers to stay in Newfoundland. Mr. Downing is said to have borne the entire cost of the expenses to carry through the litigation in London which took almost two years. A census taken in 1676 showed that St. John's had nearly 300 houses and a little over 1,000 citizens. Of all the inhabitants, the property of Mr. John Downing, with its orchard and neat vegetable and flower gardens, was considered the showplace of Old St. John's.

Down through the years the population of St. John's steadily increased. In the year 1795, the number of inhabitants of the Old Town was estimated to be nearly 4,000. Many trades sprung up to serve the public needs. The surrounding countryside had large plantations, which were cultivated farms. These properties were owned by retired naval or military officers who had obtained their land grants from the Colonial Office in London for their military services rendered to the Crown. Many of these estates became famous landmarks and places of beauty throughout the areas of suburban St. John's.

An early map of St. John's (1751) shows a plantation located on the barrens just North of Fort Townshend. This property was known as "McKie's Grove." From all reports this estate was a haven of beauty and an excellent farm. It was the centre of attraction of St. John's landscapewise in the later years of the sixteenth century. The estate was eventually purchased by Sir Hugh Emerson in or about the year 1830. Emerson built a new manor house on the land the following year. He renamed the plantation to "Belvedere." However, it was referred to by the inhabitants of Old St. John's as McKie's Grove until Bishop Fleming purchased it in 1842 for his official residence. In the year 1848, the Bishop utilized much of the back acreage as a new Catholic Cemetery and called it Belvedere. Within months the name "McKie's Grove" faded into the past. Today, two high schools (Holy Heart of Mary and Brother Rice), Belvedere (Emerson's Manor House) now St. Michael's Convent, McCauley Hall, St. Catherine's Convent, Belvedere Lodge Brother Rice Monastery and Belvedere Cemetery cover this once-great estate.

In the year 1813, the new Governor, Vice Admiral Sir Richard G. Keates K.C.B., first began the issuing of grants of land and the encouragement of agriculture to the many inhabitants of St. John's, then numbering a little more than 10,000 citizens. Before he had ended his term of administration, Sir Richard, who was the last of our migratory Governors, had issued more than 800 such land grants.

In the statistical records of the Church of England for the year 1815, there is entered the marriage of John Mitchell to Ann March on the sixth day of February of that year. The marriage was performed by the Rev. David Rowland and witnesses were Mary Anderson and Amelia Solomon. John Mitchell was a butcher of St. John's who came from Dorset England by way of Waterford, Ireland. The young man had apprenticed to the meat cutting trade and came to St. John's to work for William Thomas in the year 1810. Ann March came to St. John's with her parents as a young child in or about the year 1791. The Marches came from Devon.

After their marriage, John Mitchell went into business on his own and became successful in the butcher trade. He soon had contracts victualling the navy ships and other ships entering the port. Although he started out in provisioning these vessels with meats, he soon began supplying other produce that was grown on the farms around St. John's.

In the year 1839, John Mitchell obtained two tracts of land that were located between the then Old Portugal Cove Road on the west and the road that led to Torbay, which is today King's

Bridge Road. The land grants were bordered on the north by Rennies River and on the south by the Circular Road. This road joined the road to Torbay with the road to Portugal Cove and extended westward to connect the road to Allandale having crossed over the road that led to the Queen Victoria Hills defenses and posts, on the Burnt Pinch Trail.

At the southwest section of the property, on the smaller land grant, the Mitchells built their residence, which is known today as Bannerman House. The road leading to Portugal Cove is now named Rennies Mill Road, but the Old Circular Road still retains its original name. The date of the Mitchell residence built in the year 1840 can be seen on the chimney just above the roof line of "Bannerman House."

Mr. Mitchell used the land of the larger tract in the cultivation of root crops and an acre or so for grazing of cattle that he purchased for meat production. Around the grounds of his residence, he cultivated magnificent flower gardens which his wife and children maintained with meticulous care. Every variety of flowering seeds were cultivated. Flowers were in full bloom from late May to September in the outdoors. Later on Mrs. Mitchell had two small hothouses erected to the east side of their residence where she planted bulbs that were in bloom for Easter. She also used the houses to start seeds for outdoor planting as soon as the snows of winter had melted away and the ground was free of frost and could be cultivated.

The Mitchells sold flowers as well as farm produce. Their flower production was so prolific and beautiful that the expression "Mitchell's Gardens" came to be a favourite cant that is still in use today. Anyone walking home with a bouquet of flowers, no matter where they obtained them, could be greeted with the expression, "Oh, you must have purchased them from Mitchell's."

Whether it was for special occasions of gatherings such as the "Regatta," a key football match (an auld firm game) or a hockey game of keen competition, the event would be magnified in size or intensity by the expression, "they were there from Mitchell's." Should one be successful in showing up with a rare catch of the speckled beauties, from a May 24 excursion on return of the "Trouter's Special," someone in the crowd at the Railway Station in St. John's would be heard to utter, "Boy, he must have got them from Mitchell's," or, "such beauties, he could only have got them from Mitchell's."

The Mitchell Property passed on to the Knight Family in the year 1867. Shortly thereafter, the land that once yielded vegetables and fruit that helped feed many citizens and the varieties of flowers from "Mitchell's Gardens" that graced their homes on special occasions of Old St. John's was sold for building lots. Within years, some of the finest homes in the city sprang up in that area, many of which are in excellent condition today.

WALLACE FURLONG was born in St. John's, Newfoundland in 1918. As a young man he worked in several garages in the city before taking up responsibilities at Fort Pepperrell as an administrator of supply contracts, and eventually he retired as a land surveyor. Always interested in the history of the city, he wrote and published many articles on the people, places and events within the section of St. John's known as Georgestown. These articles were first published in the years 1980 to 1982. Wallace Furlong married Alwynne Hunter and they have two sons, Andrew and David.